THE MOBILITY WAR

MARINE CORPS HELICOPTER OPERATIONS IN VIETNAM 1962–1975

ADAM T. GIVENS, PHD

MARINES IN THE VIETNAM WAR COMMEMORATIVE SERIES

THE UNITED STATES OF AMERICA
VIETNAM WAR
SERVICE VALOR SACRIFICE
50th
COMMEMORATION

Introduction

This commemorative volume is an overview of Marine helicopters in the Vietnam War. Owing to Marine task organization and doctrine, rotary-wing aircraft were present in the Republic of Vietnam (RVN) from the start of Marine Corps involvement in the country.[1] This book's purpose is to highlight pivotal moments during more than a decade of operations. Most of these occurred in the I Corps Tactical Zone. Both a political and military region in the northernmost section of the Republic of Vietnam, it was composed of five provinces: Quang Tri, Thua Thien, Quang Nam, Quang Tin, and Quang Ngai.[2] This work presents the challenges, turning points, and issues that developed a rotary-wing capability into an invaluable asset for Marine ground operations.

The Marine helicopter commitment began as a single squadron of 24 aircraft in 1962. By the height of U.S. military involvement in the war in 1968–69, more than a dozen 1st Marine Aircraft Wing (1st MAW) helicopter squadrons were spread across three air groups were inside the RVN and two Special Landing Forces (SLF) afloat in the South China Sea. This commitment equated to half of the total number of Marine helicopters in the world.[3] Combat operations presented endless institutional, operational, and technological difficulties, but they also offered aviation leadership the opportunity to refine concepts, tactics, techniques, and procedures. The terrain and weather conditions in I Corps presented additional challenges to personnel and machinery. In the hot and dry months, dust choked gas-turbine engines and eroded rotor blades while heat and humidity diminished helicopter performance and payloads. During the monsoon season, torrential rains turned dusty airstrips into morasses and low-level clouds and precipitation tested the bravery and skills of helicopter pilots.

Vietnam was a transitional era for Marine rotary-wing aviation. The Service entered the war with dependable but aging machinery. It left with modern aircraft that served for decades and set a foundation for subsequent generations. The Marine Corps divided its helicopter inventory into multiple categories: heavy lift, medium lift, reconnaissance, utility, and attack. Sikorsky CH-53 Sea Stallions were logistical workhorses in heavy helicopter squadrons (HMH), transporting cargo and artillery pieces and rescuing stricken aircraft. Helicopters like

[1] The Republic of Vietnam is the official name of South Vietnam. This volume will use both names interchangeably.

[2] There were three tactical zones in the Republic of Vietnam initially. North to south, they were I (pronounced "Eye"), II, and III Corps. A fourth tactical zone, IV Corps, was created in November 1962 to delineate the Mekong Delta from III Corps.

[3] Report, Marine Corps Command Center, "Status of Fleet Marine Forces," 23 August 1968, Status of Forces file, Reference Branch Collection, Archives Branch, Marine Corps History Division, Quantico, VA (hereafter HD Archive), 2-1.

the Sikorsky HUS-1/UH-34D Seahorse and Boeing-Vertol CH-46 Sea Knight filled a variety of roles in medium helicopter squadrons (HMM). During combat operations, they initially served as assault vehicles for ground combat elements, ferrying troops between base areas and the field, before shifting to supplying units with crucial supplies, including ammunition, food, water, and mail. If ground forces made contact with the enemy, medium helicopter crews flew casualty evacuation missions (casevac), removing the wounded and dead from the battlefield.

Marine doctrine before Vietnam prescribed the role of close air support to fixed-wing aircraft.[4] The unique demands of combat in Vietnam, however, made armed helicopters crucial to infantry operations. Marines came to rely on them to protect transport aircraft and rapidly provide close air support to ground combat elements. Although the Marine Corps initially procured the Bell UH-1E "Huey" in 1962 as an assault support helicopter, before its introduction to the inventory it became additionally configured as a gunship, mirroring the U.S. Army's use of its UH-1s in that role. The eventual arrival of the Bell AH-1G Cobra in 1969, the first attack helicopter in the Marine Corps inventory, gave Marines even greater firepower.

Helicopters played an integral role in the Marine Corps' air-ground concept of aviation assets during the Vietnam War, assisting ground operations in combat, reconnaissance, transportation, and supply. That concept stretches back to the first Marine aviators in 1912. Marine Aviation became a formal component of the air-ground team in 1933 with the creation of the Fleet Marine Force (FMF).[5] Title 10 of the U.S. Code establishes the air-ground concept in law and stipulates that the Marine Corps is organized to provide Fleet Marineforces of combined arms with supporting air components.[6] This teamwork served as the foundation of the Marine way of warfare in Southeast Asia, an approach that coordinated ground, air, and logistics that endures today.

The Marine Corps and Helicopters, 1946–62

The Marine Corps was at the forefront of military helicopter development in the years following World War II. Its rotary-wing program officially began when it commissioned Marine Helicopter Squadron 1 (HMX-1) in 1947 at Quantico, Virginia. Helicopter design was still in its first generation, the product of hobby inventors struggling to expand beyond the scale of a cottage industry. Igor Sikorsky produced the first successful American-built helicopter in 1939. His Bridgeport, Connecticut, firm turned out more than 400 aircraft for the U.S. military before the end of World War II.[7]

Manufacturers such as Bell Aircraft and Piasecki Helicopter led the field with Sikorsky through the rest of the decade. Faced with dismal commercial prospects after the war, most of the U.S. aircraft industry sought potentially lucrative military contracts.[8] As a result, government-funded research and development contributed to early advancements in rotary-wing technology. Helicopters lacked power and size in the 1940s, which initially limited military applications and restricted planning. By the latter part of the decade, however, larger and more capable designs broadened operational possibilities.

The Marine Corps was an early adopter of the nascent technology and began evaluating rotary-wing aircraft in 1946.[9] Its search for technological solutions to deal with the new atomic battlefield ultimately led to the founding of the helicopter program a year later. Marine planners realized that atomic weapons made amphibious operations increasingly vulnerable, as even a small number of bombs could destroy an expeditionary force.[10] Aviation-minded planners supported a new concept for amphibious operations that used helicopters, called "vertical assault."[11] Flying troops from the decks of U.S.

[4] See Robert Sherrod, *History of Marine Corps Aviation in World War II* (Washington, DC: Combat Forces Press, 1952), 31–33; and MajGen John P. Condon, USMC (Ret), and Cmdr Peter B. Mersky, USN (Ret), *Corsairs to Panthers: U.S. Marine Aviation in Korea* (Washington, DC: U.S. Marine Corps Historical Center, 2002), 4–5.

[5] See LtCol Edward C. Johnson, *Marine Corps Aviation: The Early Years, 1912–1940*, ed. Graham A. Cosmas (Washington, DC: History and Museums Division, Headquarters, U.S. Marine Corps, 1977), 61–65.

[6] U.S. Code, Title 10—Section 8063, United States Marine Corps: composition; functions (1956).

[7] *Hearing before the United States Senate Special Committee on Investigating the National Defense Program, Seventy-Ninth Congress, First Session, Part 32, 21 September 1945* (Washington, DC: Government Printing Office, 1946), 16396.

[8] "Survey Shows Slump in Aircraft Sales," *Aviation Week* 48, no. 15 (12 April 1948): 18.

[9] LtCol Eugene W. Rawlins, USMC, *Marines and Helicopters, 1946–1962*, ed. Maj William J. Sambito, USMC (Washington, DC: History and Museums Division, Headquarters, U.S. Marine Corps, 1976), 11.

[10] As quoted in Rawlins, *Marines and Helicopters, 1946–1962*, 11.

[11] Rawlins, *Marines and Helicopters, 1946–1962*, 38–39.

Navy ships promised increased combat power projection in a new era of warfare.

As Marines later understood in Vietnam, it was not the technological feat of helicopters that made them consequential. Rather, the mobility they provided was the significant factor. It was up to Marine helicopter pioneers to determine how best to utilize the mobility of helicopters as part of air-ground integration. Freed of the restrictions of reefs, surf, and beach defenses with which landing craft had to contend, rotary-wing aircraft offered flexibility, speed, and rapid concentration of forces. They theoretically allowed both dispersion and rapid concentration of forces. Launching from aircraft carriers, loads of assault troops would act as the initial attack waves in an amphibious operation. Helicopters could rapidly deploy infantry beyond prepared enemy defensive positions and link ship and shore, ferrying supplies and personnel, evacuating casualties, and repositioning troops for continuing operations.

In 1947, HMX-1 used tentative doctrine that the Marine Corps Schools developed to test and study the employment of helicopters in amphibious operations.[12] By 1950, the unit developed tactics and techniques and demonstrated the utility of rotary-wing mobility. Operational experience during the Korean War helped refine the concept. Within weeks of the war's start, a small detachment of officers and Marines joined Marine Observation Squadron 6 (VMO-6) as part of Marine Aircraft Group 33 (MAG-33). Flying four Sikorsky HO3S-1s (S-48s), the first squadron reorganized to include helicopters in combat missions. The Marine Corps also commissioned its first transport helicopter squadron, Marine Helicopter Transport Squadron 161 (HMR-161), and sent it to Korea in the summer of 1951 with the dual purpose of testing and evaluating the new Sikorsky HSR (S-55) helicopter in an operational environment and supporting the 1st Marine Division[13]

The helicopter program expanded rapidly during the war, but budget austerity during President Dwight D. Eisenhower's first administration forced it into a period of developmental stasis. Hindered by limited funding but still committed to what was now termed the vertical envelopment concept, the Marine Corps altered its organizations and tactics to align with available rotary-wing technology.[14] Planners based doctrine and force structure around the large Sikorsky HR2S, but it proved too bulky and expensive and did not perform to expectations. The Marines revised their vertical envelopment concept around available helicopter technology, which meant lighter and smaller aircraft.[15] By 1956, nine squadrons of the multipurpose HRS transport helicopters made up the bulk of the vertical envelopment aviation force, a total of 180 aircraft.[16] These strategic, funding, and technological factors ultimately produced the somewhat light and mobile force that the Marine Corps deployed to Vietnam.

Deployment to Southeast Asia

By 1961, RVN president Ngo Dinh Diem and his government faced a growing crisis in the country as Communists and other antigovernment elements waged an insurgency that escalated into a civil war. The National Liberation Front (NLF), a South Vietnamese Communist revolutionary organization allied with Hanoi, aimed to overthrow the government in Saigon and reunify the country. It controlled, directed, and coordinated the revolutionary movement in the south. Its military arm, the Viet Cong, received materiel support from the Democratic Republic of Vietnam (DRV) and fought as guerrillas, intimidating the population, sabotaging government programs, and using hit-and-run tactics against South Vietnamese forces.[17] Utilizing Mao Zedong's concept of the "people's war," the Viet Cong preferred quick platoon- or company-size strikes against

[12] Rawlins, *Marines and Helicopters, 1946–1962*, 14–21.

[13] Rawlins, *Marines and Helicopters, 1946–1962*, 25–51.

[14] Carl John Horn III, "Military Innovation and the Helicopter: A Comparison of Development in the United States Army and Marine Corps, 1945–1965" (PhD diss., Ohio State University, 2004), 136–68.

[15] Horn, "Military Innovation and the Helicopter," 167–68.

[16] Horn, "Military Innovation and the Helicopter," 148.

[17] The term *Viet Cong* is a colloquialism meaning "Vietnamese Communist" that originated in the 1920s to differentiate the group from Chinese Communists. While some groups have assigned pejorative value to the term, it is used here purely as a descriptive identifier. The organization is also known as the Liberation Army of South Vietnam and the People's Liberation Armed Forces (not to be confused with the People's Republic of China's armed forces, known as the People's Liberation Army). See Brett Reilly, "The True Origin of the Term 'Viet Cong'," *Diplomat*, 31 January 2018. The Democratic Republic of Vietnam is the official name of North Vietnam. This volume will use both names interchangeably.

government-allied villages or isolated outposts. Engagements lasted less than 15 minutes on average.[18]

For President John F. Kennedy's administration, which prioritized counterinsurgency in policy planning, South Vietnamese security was a regional problem—insurgency there could theoretically destabilize Southeast Asia if not properly countered.[19] The political situation deteriorated as Communist fighters infiltrated the south; in two years, the Viet Cong's strength in the RVN grew five-fold.[20] President Kennedy sent White House military representative U.S. Army General Maxwell D. Taylor along with Deputy National Security Advisor Walt W. Rostow to the Republic of Vietnam in October 1961 to find ways of "urgently improving the effectiveness" of the South Vietnamese military, "including the rapid provision of additional equipment, manned if necessary by U.S. personnel."[21]

Helicopters were at the vanguard of U.S. intervention in the RVN as part of larger strategic calculations. While Diem requested troops to protect cities and villages, Taylor believed offensive operations were less expensive and more promising than defensive ones. Among Taylor's many conclusions in his report to Kennedy, he recommended providing South Vietnam additional aviation support, including three helicopter units, to take back the initiative from the Communists.[22] To his mind, "an effective operation against the Viet-Cong requires ample air supply, as well as ample troop-lift capacity."[23] This meant Army of the Republic of Vietnam (ARVN) units and South Vietnamese Marines reacting quicker in attack and defense against highly mobile guerrilla bands.[24]

As Army chief of staff during the 1950s, Taylor had been a vocal proponent of using helicopters in brushfire wars. He reasoned at the time that rotary-wing aircraft could "do for us in the air what trucks do for us on the ground."[25] Helicopters seemed to offer a solution to the problem of countering elusive and quick-striking enemy fighters. Rotary-wing technology might give RVN forces the opportunity to regain the offensive, allowing the South Vietnamese military to reach into the provinces where the Viet Cong operated.[26] Military successes would also mean protecting the rural population who lived in fear of the Communists, possibly boosting confidence in the government.[27]

The difficulties presented by an enemy who could mass, attack, and disappear swiftly were made more difficult by the country's rough terrain, long distances between populated areas, and lack of a sophisticated national infrastructure.[28] The Republic of Vietnam had only about 4,000 kilometers of all-weather roads at the time. The primary north-south artery, Route 1, connected coastal villages, but there were few developed roads inland. The lack of adequate means of communication was noticeable after leaving Saigon, as travelers entered a vast rural expanse. The country in 1962 had a population of 14 million, but only about 10 percent lived in urban communities.[29] Hamlets dotted the countryside while larger towns acted as government-controlled centers in the rural areas. Thirty kilometers northeast of Saigon was the major suburb of Bien Hoa, while the port city of Vung Tau

[18] Marine Corps Operations Analysis Group, "Study No. 1, Characteristics of U.S. Marine Corps Helicopter Operations in the Mekong Delta, 1962," 12 March 1963, box 5, folder 10, Vietnam Helicopter Pilots Association (VHPA) Collection, item no. 2930510001, The Vietnam Center and Sam Johnson Vietnam Archive, Texas Tech University, Lubbock, TX (hereafter TTU Vietnam Archive), 11.

[19] Ingo Trauschweizer, *Maxwell Taylor's Cold War: From Berlin to Vietnam* (Lexington: University Press of Kentucky, 2019), 119.

[20] Lawrence S. Kaplan, Ronald D. Landa, and Edward J. Drea, *History of the Office of the Secretary of Defense*, vol. 5, *The McNamara Ascendancy, 1961–1965* (Washington, DC: Historical Office, Office of the Secretary of Defense, 2006), 270.

[21] As quoted in Trauschweizer, *Maxwell Taylor's Cold War*, 120.

[22] Trauschweizer, *Maxwell Taylor's Cold War*, 121.

[23] "210. Letter from the President's Military Representative (Taylor) to the President," in *Foreign Relations of the United States, 1961–1963*, vol. 1, *Vietnam, 1961*, ed. Ronald D. Landa and Charles S. Sampson (Washington, DC: Government Printing Office, 1988), 496.

[24] Official U.S. Marine Corps documents typically do not capitalize the occupation of foreign military personnel (e.g., soldier, sailor, or marine); however, the term "Marines" will be capitalized throughout when referring to members of a foreign military service (e.g., South Vietnamese Marines) to align with MCUP style.

[25] Address by Gen Maxwell D. Taylor, USA, to the National Press Club, Washington, DC, 3 April 1956, Maxwell D. Taylor Papers, National Defense University Digital Archive, 7. See also Gen Maxwell D. Taylor, "The Changing Army," *Army Combat Forces Journal* 6, no. 3 (October 1955): 10; and Ingo Trauschweizer, *The Cold War U.S. Army: Building Deterrence for Limited War* (Lawrence: University Press of Kansas, 2008), 58–61.

[26] BGen Delk M. Oden, USA, *U.S. Army Aviation Operations in South Vietnam* (Washington, DC: Office of the Deputy Chief of Staff for Military Operations, Department of the Army, 1962), 4–5.

[27] Trauschweizer, *Maxwell Taylor's Cold War*, 121.

[28] Oden, *U.S. Army Aviation Operations in South Vietnam*, 4–5.

[29] *U.S. Army Area Handbook for Vietnam* (Washington, DC: Department of the Army, 1962), 31–32.

SOUTH VIETNAM CORPS TACTICAL ZONES

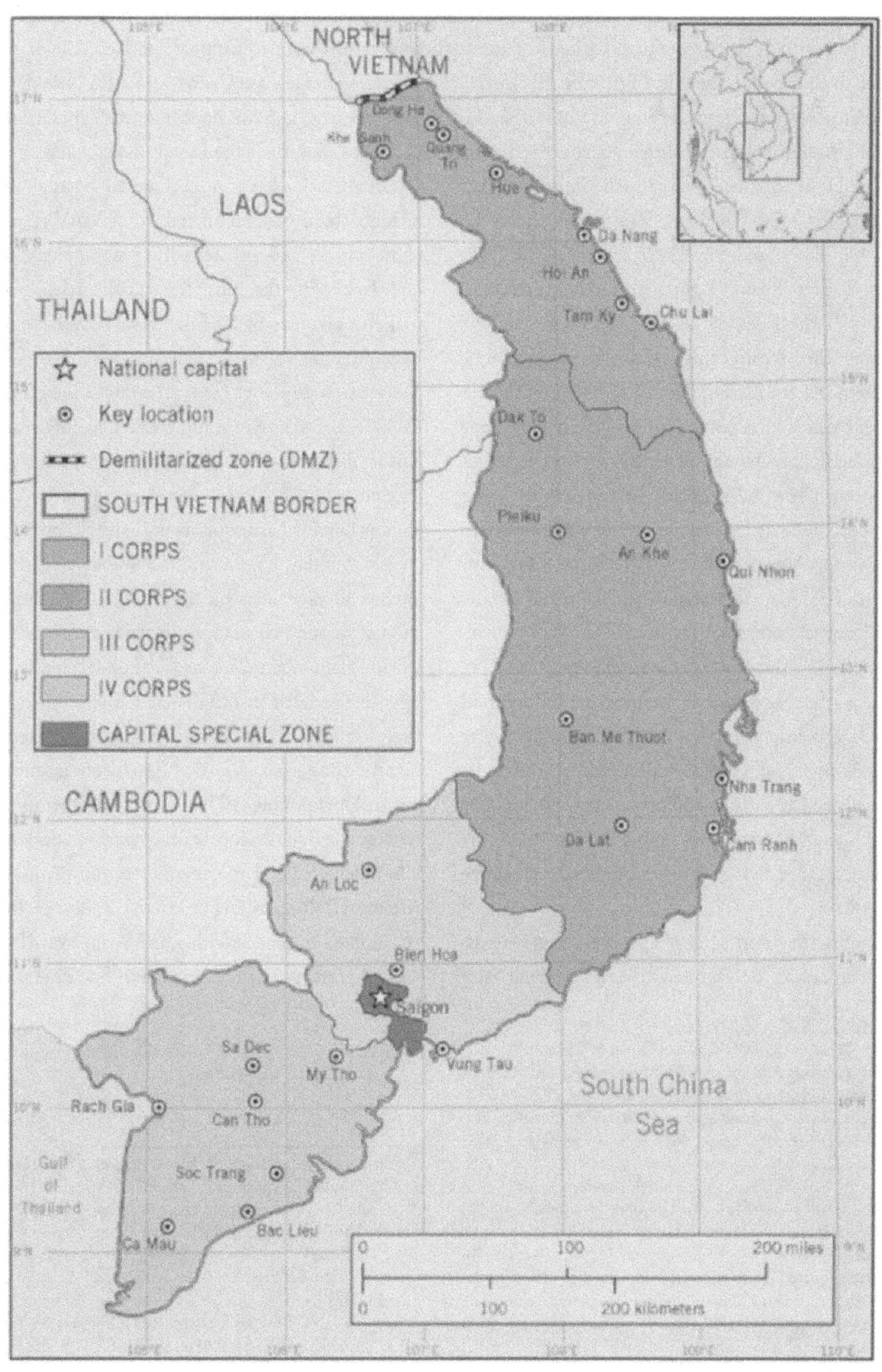

Map courtesy of Pete McPhail, adapted by MCUP

clung to the coastline. One-hundred thirty kilometers southwest of Saigon lay Can Tho, with My Tho roughly between the two.[30]

Kennedy agreed with Taylor's recommendation to deploy helicopter units to South Vietnam. The first came from the U.S. Army's Transportation Corps, arriving at Saigon on 11 December 1961.[31] The initial three companies, equipped with Boeing-Vertol CH-21 Shawnee cargo helicopters, proved so successful that the Joint Chiefs of Staff requested on 17 January 1962 that Commander in Chief, Pacific (CinCPac), Admiral Harry D. Felt review the total requirements for U.S. military support of the Republic of Vietnam. Admiral Felt recommended another Army company deploy to Southeast Asia to operate in the southern region of the country, in the Mekong River Delta.[32] The commanding general of Fleet Marine Force, Pacific, Lieutenant General Alan Shapley, suggested a Marine squadron of 24 HUS-1 Seahorses replace one of the Army companies in the coastal city of Da Nang, the center of gravity for American forces in I Corps.[33] General Paul D. Harkins, U.S. Army commander of the newly established U.S. Military Command, Vietnam (USMACV)—the central headquarters of the American military effort in Vietnam, based in Saigon—agreed with the proposal but lobbied for the Marine squadron to operate in the Mekong Delta instead.[34] The Army's 93d Transportation Company (Light Helicopter) only recently became operational at Da Nang. For it to move south would decrease its support just as the monsoon season ended there, flying weather improved, and operational tempo increased.

On 16 March, the Joint Chiefs approved the plan to send a Marine squadron to Vietnam. The 1st Marine Aircraft Wing—tasked with supporting Navy and Marine Corps air operations in the Western Pacific, including Vietnam—selected HMM-362 to deploy to the RVN. The squadron's orders were to support the Republic of Vietnam's Civil Guard, Self-Defense Corps, and ARVN soldiers. Designated Task Force 79.3.5 but code-named "Operation Shufly" (pronounced "shoe-fly"), the squadron activated on 4 April 1962.[35]

Three task elements comprised Shufly. The task force's headquarters, which reported to 1st MAW, consisted of six to eight officers and enlisted. The second element was HMM-362. To increase flexibility, the squadron deployed with its normal complement of 24 Sikorsky HUS-1 medium-lift cargo helicopters as well as 3 single-engine Cessna OE-1 Bird Dog observation airplanes from Marine Observation Squadron 2 (VMO-2) and a twin-engine Douglas R4D cargo aircraft for liaison and supply flights.[36] Shufly's final piece was Sub Unit 2, an element from Marine Air Base Squadron 16 (MABS-16), responsible for base support and airfield operations.[37]

On Sunday, 15 April, USS *Princeton* (LPH 5) dropped anchor 30 kilometers off the Republic of Vietnam's coast. "As soon as we stepped out topside we knew we were in a different world," remembered Lance Corporal Tyler K. Bush, an intelligence specialist in HMM-362. Even out on the darkened flight deck it "was so intense and muggy it felt like trying to breathe through a pillow."[38] Squadron commander Lieutenant Colonel Archie J. Clapp initiated Operation Shufly when he flew the first helicopter off *Princeton*'s deck and traveled 50 kilometers to a 900-meter concrete runway in the heart of the Mekong Delta, arriving at HMM-362's new home at 0730.[39] A Japanese fighter base during World War II, the facility lay 4 kilometers south of the village of Soc Trang, 135 kilometers

[30] Capt Robert H. Whitlow, USMCR, *U.S. Marines in Vietnam: The Advisory and Combat Assistance Era, 1954–1964* (Washington, DC: History and Museums Division, Headquarters, U.S. Marine Corps, 1977), 62.

[31] Maj B. D. Harper, USA, *Logistical Support of Airmobile Operations, Republic of Vietnam (1961–1971)* (St. Louis, MO: U.S. Army Aviation Systems Command, 1971), 1–6.

[32] LtCol William R. Fails, USMC, *Marines and Helicopters, 1962–1973* (Washington, DC: History and Museums Division, Headquarters, U.S. Marine Corps, 1978), 28.

[33] The Department of Defense's Tri-Service aircraft designation system in November 1962 redesignated many aircraft, including the HUS-1 to the UH-34D. To avoid anachronisms, this volume uses the period-correct terminology where appropriate—HUS-1 before November 1962, UH-34D after.

[34] Dick Camp, *Assault from the Sky: U.S. Marine Corps Helicopter Operations in Vietnam* (Philadelphia: Casemate Publishers, 2013), 15.

[35] Whitlow, *The Advisory and Combat Assistance Era, 1954–1964*, 57–59.

[36] Whitlow, *The Advisory and Combat Assistance Era, 1954–1964*, 60.

[37] Marine Corps Operations Analysis Group, "Study No. 1 Characteristics of U.S. Marine Corps Helicopter Operations in the Mekong Delta, 1962," 3.

[38] Tyler K. Bush, "Vietnam—25 Years Ago," *Leatherneck* 70, no. 8 (August 1987): 34.

[39] Summary of CTU 79.3.5 Operations [Commander Task Unit of 79.3.5, a.k.a. "Shufly"], 9–26 April 1962, folder 67, U.S. Marine Corps History Division Vietnam War Documents Collection, item no. 1201067185, TTU Vietnam Archive, 2.

Procuring the Sikorsky HUS-1/UH-34D

U.S. Navy planners originally considered the HUS-1 Seahorse to be an interim aircraft until the development and production of large assault helicopters became technologically feasible. The Navy procured it in 1954 as the HSS-1 Sea Bat, an antisubmarine helicopter. However, helicopter proponents within the U.S. Army and the Marine Corps saw the aircraft's potential in a utility role. With more than twice the load-carrying capability of the Sikorsky HRS that had been in service with the Marine Corps since the Korean War, the HSS-1 had the ability to carry troops internally as well as cargo both internally or sling-loaded externally.

Removing submarine-hunting equipment from the HSS-1 freed up much-needed room and shed 340 pounds from the Navy variant for the Marine-designated HUS-1. To address its new role as a utility helicopter capable of logistical and assault functions, Seahorses featured reinforced floors below and behind the pilots with additional tie-down points to secure cargo. Adding a step underneath the main door allowed troops to load and unload faster. In total, the Marine Corps procured approximately 540 aircraft. In November 1962, in compliance with Department of Defense aircraft redesignations, the HUS-1 became the UH-34D, or "Dog," as the Marines affectionately referred to it.[1]

[1] LtCol William R. Fails, USMC, *Marines and Helicopters, 1962–1973* (Washington, DC: History and Museums Division, Headquarters, U.S. Marine Corps, 1978), 5–6; Dick Camp, *Assault from the Sky: U.S. Marine Corps Helicopter Operations in Vietnam* (Philadelphia: Casemate Publishers, 2013), 15; and Col Bob Stoffey, *Cleared Hot!: A Marine Combat Pilot's Vietnam Diary* (New York: St. Martin's Press, 1992), 25.

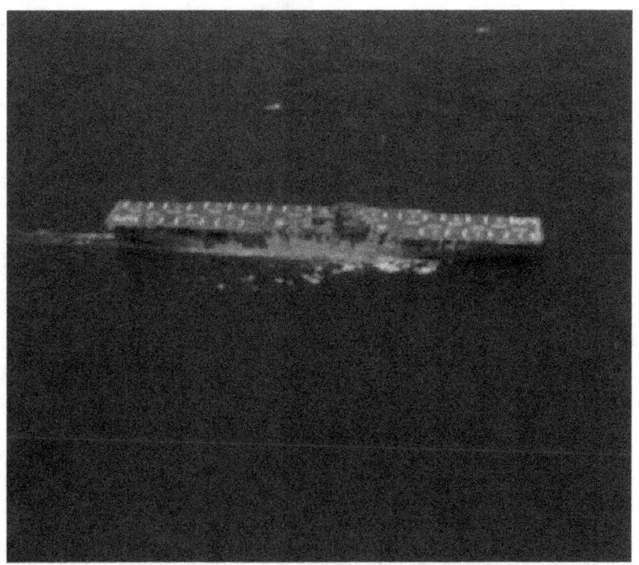

Warren Smith Collection, Archives Branch, Marine Corps History Division

HUS-1s on board USS *Princeton*.

southwest of Saigon, in the III Corps Tactical Zone.[40] With the help of HMM-261, HMM-362 flew more than 200 sorties between *Princeton* and Soc Trang by 1700 hours on the first day, moving 264 personnel and 200,000 pounds of cargo.[41]

With only two permanent buildings at Soc Trang—a dilapidated hanger and a structure that became the mess hall—the Marines attempted to improve living conditions and conveniences.[42] They erected 75 tents, assembled a water purification system, built a field laundry and post office, and wired telephones.[43] Two ARVN battalions provided perimeter security while Marines from the squadron manned internal defenses. HMM-362 was operational within 24 hours. Quick preparation of the airfield at Soc Trang supported sustained operations within two weeks.[44]

[40] This area of operations would later become IV Corps, after the government of the Republic of Vietnam and USMACV created that new tactical zone in November 1962. This work refers to where Shufly operated as III Corps, as that is the historically accurate term for the period of time covered here.

[41] Summary of CTU 79.3.5 Operations, 9–26 April 1962, 2.

[42] David H. Hugel, "Colonel Archive J. Clapp: A Marine Corps Aviation Legend," *Leatherneck* 92, no. 10 (October 2009): 44.

[43] Whitlow, *The Advisory and Combat Assistance Era, 1954–1964*, 62.

[44] Bush, "Vietnam—25 Years Ago," 34; and Whitlow, *The Advisory and Combat Assistance Era, 1954–1964*, 63.

MEKONG DELTA, 1962

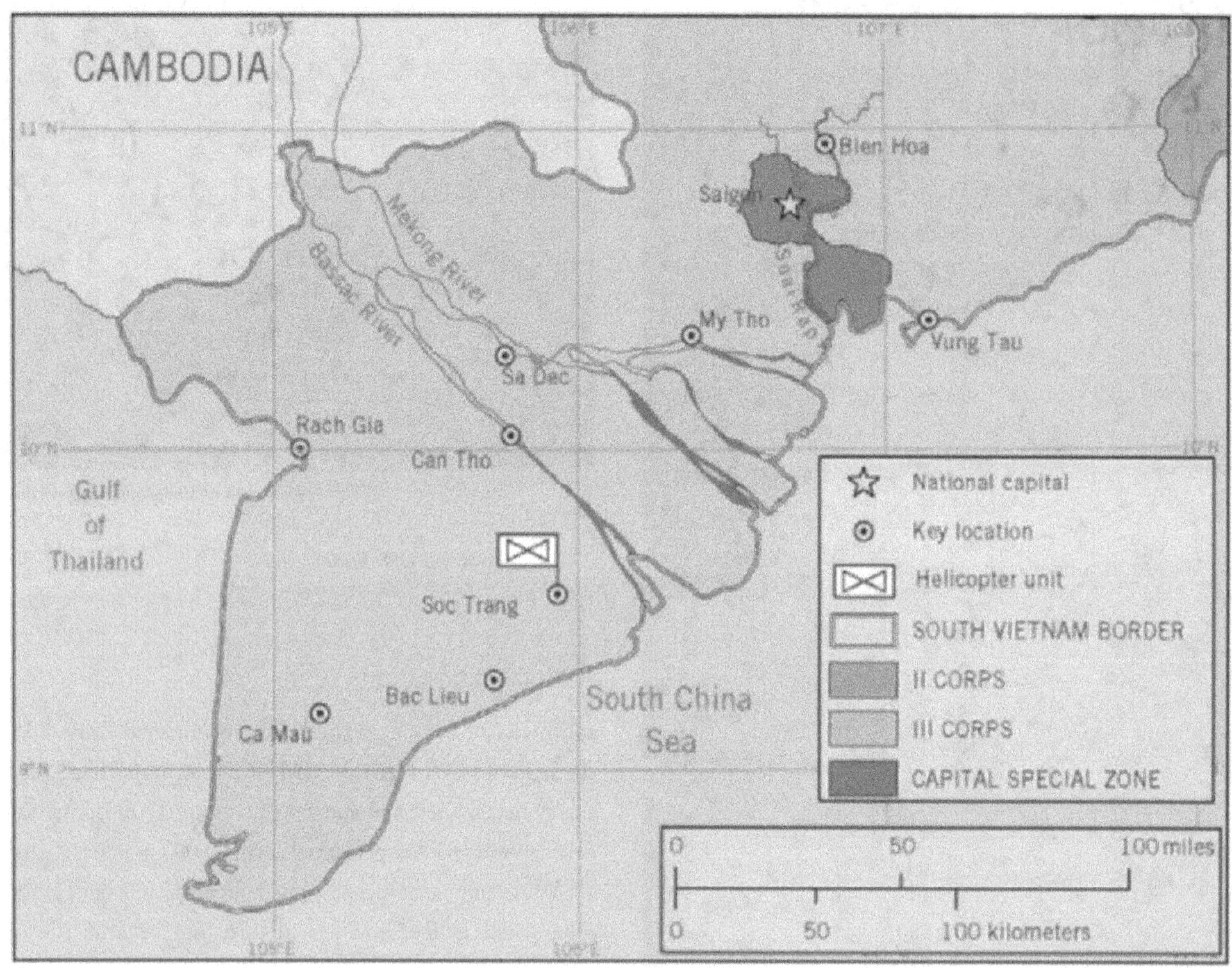

Map courtesy of Pete McPhail, adapted by MCUP

Early Operations

HMM-362 flew its first tactical troop lift mission in the Mekong Delta during Operation Lockjaw on 22 April. Alongside the U.S. Army's Saigon-based 57th Transportation Company (Light Helicopter), Lieutenant Colonel Clapp led 16 Shufly HUS-1s in transporting 339 troops from the 7th ARVN Division. The next day, the squadron lifted South Vietnamese Marines near the southern tip of the Republic of Vietnam to evacuate a government outpost.[45] The Shufly Marines faced only light opposition and received no damage from enemy fire. Although there were regular reminders that they were involved in a war, they initially remained in an advisory role and did not fly at night or on weekends.[46] After three weeks in-country, the task force boasted it was becoming what it considered "a very potent thorn in the side of Mekong Delta guerrillas."[47]

[45] After Action Report, Marine Task Unit 79.3.5, Mission Order Number 5, 21 April 1962, HD Archive.

[46] Gregg Jones, *Last Stand at Khe Sanh: The U.S. Marines' Finest Hour in Vietnam* (Boston, MA: Da Capo Press, 2014), 197.

[47] Summary of CTU 79.3.5 Operations, 9–26 April 1962, 1–2.

Developing Tactics and Doctrine

The amphibious capability around which the Marines based their vertical envelopment concept was mostly absent during Shufly. The task force's land-based character was a departure from prescribed doctrine. However, fighting in Vietnam offered a way for the Marines to test recent doctrinal theories and find the operational limits of the HUS-1.[48] With greater power and a carrying capacity of between 8 to 12 combat-loaded troops, HUS-1s were capable of hauling more personnel and cargo than the smaller Sikorsky HRSs. These testing efforts were not casual or ad hoc. The 1st MAW specifically developed and assessed tactics and equipment with an eye toward improving the effectiveness of helicopter operations.[49] Under Lieutenant Colonel Clapp's leadership, "Archie's Angels," as the Marines of HMM-362 referred to themselves, refined tactics and doctrine in late spring 1962, setting the standards for Marine heliborne operations in the Republic of Vietnam and becoming the archetype for the Shufly squadrons that followed.[50]

In the first year of Shulfy operations, a typical helicopter combat assault took place on average every two days and involved 14 helicopters. Planners plotted courses between the loading and landing zones (LZ), usually 12–30 kilometers apart, which avoided populated areas. Pilots considered dry rice paddies the best landing zones because they were flat and free of obstacles. Their chosen routes featured landmarks in the final 15 kilometers of the strike, which pilots could identify when flying at only 3 to 5 meters above the ground to avoid enemy ground fire. When possible, flight leaders reconnoitered the designated LZs the day before an operation to familiarize themselves with the area and confirm the plan's suitability. During the strike, an observation airplane loitered above the standard formation of four helicopters, relaying heading corrections and an estimated distance remaining to the site.[51]

Flying from Soc Trang required crews to transit an average of 80 kilometers to loading points, where Republic of Vietnam troops climbed aboard, then another 30 kilometers to the landing zone. A typical operation required anywhere from one to four lifts to shuttle troops and supplies into the LZs.[52] The first operations in April 1962 revealed that local militia from the Self-Defense Corps did not board or exit aircraft efficiently enough. Helicopters spending excessive time either hovering or sitting on the ground increased the risk of drawing enemy fire. To reduce their exposure in landing zones, HMM-362 and militia members conducted training after Operation Lockjaw in how to "embark, sit, signal, and debark" the helicopters. The result, the squadron reported, was a "smooth running [*sic*], expeditious operation."[53]

Viet Cong fighters seldom engaged helicopter assaults during the task force's first year. They chose instead to shelter in hideouts or blend into the civilian population, frustrating the ARVN.[54] When the Viet Cong did target Marine helicopters, they occasionally scored hits. Shufly Marines had little practical knowledge of how their helicopters would stand up to the rigors of combat. They discovered that while their airframes were rugged, vital components such as engines, transmissions, and tail rotor gear boxes were vulnerable and required armor plating. The squadron learned this only nine days after arriving at Soc Trang, when enemy ground fire severed an engine oil line and forced an HUS-1 to make an emergency landing. Constables from the nearby city of Can Tho provided security while the crew repaired the helicopter and flew back to Soc Trang.[55] Despite these vulnerabilities, most Marine crews were impressed by the ability of their aircraft to absorb damage and return home.[56]

The Viet Cong were quick to recognize and exploit patterns in Marine and ARVN techniques, tactics, and procedures. In a

[48] "Letter of Instruction, Shufly," 12 November 1962, enc. 2, letter from commanding general (CG) of 1st Marine Aircraft Wing (1st MAW), 5 September 1963, folder 67, U.S. Marine Corps History Division Vietnam War Documents Collection, item no. 1201067185, TTU Vietnam Archive, 1.

[49] "Letter of Instruction, Shufly" (12 November 1962), 1.

[50] Robert B. Asprey, "Saga at Soc Trang: Marines in Viet-Nam," *Marine Corps Gazette* 46, no. 12 (December 1962): 2.

[51] Weekly Summary [1st MAW], 13–19 May 1962, folder 67, U.S. Marine Corps History Division Vietnam War Documents Collection, item no. 1201067185, TTU Vietnam Archive, 3–4.

[52] Marine Corps Operations Analysis Group, "Study No. 1, Characteristics of U.S. Marine Corps Helicopter Operations in the Mekong Delta, 1962," 5–10, 16.

[53] After Action Report, Marine Task Unit 79.3.5, Mission Order Number 6, 21 April 1962, HD Archive.

[54] Marine Corps Operations Analysis Group, "Study No. 1, Characteristics of U.S. Marine Corps Helicopter Operations in the Mekong Delta, 1962," 11.

[55] After Action Report, Marine Task Unit 79.3.5, Mission Order Number 14, 23 April 1962, HD Archive.

[56] *USMC/Vietnam Helicopter Association: Pop a Smoke* (Paducah, KY: Turner Publishing Company, 2001), 26.

Archie J. Clapp Collection,
Archives Branch, Marine Corps History Division

UH-34Ds from HMM-362 deliver an ARVN company during an early Shufly mission, July 1962.

Defense Department (Marine Corps) A420828

LtCol Archie Clapp delivers a predawn briefing to HMM-362 pilots on 26 July 1962.

typical assault during the first year, Republic of Vietnam Air Force (RVNAF) fixed-wing aircraft prepared landing zones with air strikes just prior to the arrival of the helicopters. This revealed the location of the LZs and gave enemy fighters time to prepare a hasty ambush. As a result, the RVNAF escorted Marine helicopters with Douglas AD-6 Skyraider attack aircraft or North American T-28 Trojan light-attack aircraft.[57] Meanwhile, Marine Cessna OE-1 or ARVN Cessna L-19 observation aircraft loitered above the battlefield, relaying information to ARVN soldiers about enemy locations, marking objects to orient ground troops, and guiding helicopters.[58]

Early on, when the ARVN located the enemy, it often took too long to engage them. In response, Shufly developed fast reaction missions as a way to speed up response times and take advantage of opportunities when they arose. Lieutenant Colonel Clapp and Colonel John F. Carey, the task group commander, developed "Eagle Flights," a new concept named for the bird of prey's method of striking its quarry quickly from above. Working with ground elements, these missions typically consisted of four helicopters with nearly 50 ARVN troops that loitered until needed. After a ground commander or an OE-1 pilot located the enemy, the helicopters delivered the airborne reserves to blocking positions to cut off the fighters' escape.[59] The delta's flat terrain often offered numerous landing zones for the entire flight of helicopters to land quickly and deploy the troops.

Shufly ran its first quick reaction mission on 18 June during a large ground operation. Within a month, Marines considered Eagle Flights a sound concept worth continued use. The method appeared to have a positive impact on the tactical situation in the Mekong Delta, in that it typically generated contact with the enemy. Eagle Flights forced guerrilla elements to engage South Vietnamese ground units more often than at any point thus far in the war, and in several operations it was the principal means of killing, wounding, or capturing Communist fighters.[60] Marines and U.S. Army units used variants of the tactic throughout the war under different monikers, such as Tiger Flight, Sparrow Hawk, Chickenhawk, Pacifier, and Quick Reaction Force.[61]

[57] The Trojans, for example, carried 2.75-inch rockets, napalm canisters, bombs between 100 and 1,000 pounds, a 20-millimeter cannon, and .50-caliber machine guns. Whitlow, *The Advisory and Combat Assistance Era, 1954–1964*, 65.

[58] Marine Corps Operations Analysis Group, "Study No. 1, Characteristics of U.S. Marine Corps Helicopter Operations in the Mekong Delta, 1962," 14.

[59] Whitlow, *The Advisory and Combat Assistance Era, 1954–1964*, 69.

[60] Marine Corps Operations Analysis Group, "Study No. 1, Characteristics of U.S. Marine Corps Helicopter Operations in the Mekong Delta, 1962," 17.

[61] Whitlow, *The Advisory and Combat Assistance Era, 1954–1964*, 69.

People's Liberation Armed Forces of Southern Vietnam

The People's Liberation Armed Forces of Southern Vietnam, or Viet Cong ("Vietnamese Communists"), was the official military arm of the National Liberation Front. It operated a well-organized military and political insurgency in the Republic of Vietnam, answering to military authorities in the Democratic Republic of Vietnam.[1] The Communists relied on rural workers, the overwhelming majority of the population in Vietnam, to fill the ranks. Recruiting efforts at the village and hamlet levels, especially in the Mekong Delta, appealed to a large percentage of people who had grievances against the South Vietnamese government.

Through the early 1960s, the Hanoi-sanctioned revolutionary struggle remained in the initial stage of guerrilla warfare. While it openly controlled about 10 percent of the hamlets in the Republic of Vietnam, the Viet Cong reportedly enjoyed influence over another 60 percent of the villages and could access at least one-quarter of the nation's men of military age. In early 1960, the insurgency numbered 4,000 fighters. By the time the Shufly Marines arrived, the Viet Cong were more than 20,000 strong, organized into 20 battalions, 80 separate companies, and as many as 100 platoons.[2] Using assassination and terrorism, the insurgency gained traction by early 1962.

Unlike popular stereotypes in the West, which characterized the Viet Cong as poorly equipped peasants who farmed by day and picked up crude weapons at night, the reality is more sophisticated. There were three distinct Viet Cong factions, similar in design to the Chinese National Revolutionary Army:

- Main force units were made up of professional soldiers from both North and South Vietnam. The soldiers received training in the Democratic Republic of Vietnam before infiltrating south, and its leadership came from the Central Office for South Vietnam (COSVN), Hanoi's agency that coordinated Communist activities in the Republic of Vietnam. Main force units were capable of operating throughout South Vietnam and were often employed during major attacks. Equipped with arms either carried from the north or captured from the South Vietnamese military, they were organized along the same lines as the battalion-regiment-division arrangement of conventional forces.
- Regionally based local-force units were full-time fighters who were reasonably trained, equipped, and educated but not to the same degree as their main-force comrades. They operated locally in companies or platoons, responding to district- and provincial-level authorities, and were made up of a mixture of guerrillas and insurgents from organized commands.
- The third faction, part-time village guerrillas or militia detachments, operated in small units under the command of local Communist committees. Although not adept fighters, they were valuable as intelligence gatherers and guides for main-force units.[3]

[1] Pierre Asselin, *Vietnam's American War: A History* (New York: Cambridge University Press, 2018), 103.

[2] Graham A. Cosmas, *MACV: The Joint Command in the Years of Withdrawal, 1968–1973* (Washington, DC: Center of Military History, United States Army, 2006), 72.

[3] Warren Wilkins, *Grab Their Belts to Fight Them: The Viet Cong's Big Unit War Against the U.S., 1965–1966* (Annapolis, MD: Naval Institute Press, 2011), 15; Cosmas, *MACV: The Joint Command in the Years of Withdrawal, 1968–1973*, 72-73; Col George R. Hofmann Jr., USMCR, *Path to War: U.S. Marine Corps Operations in Southeast Asia, 1961 to 1965*, Marines in the Vietnam War Commemorative Series (Quantico, VA: Marine Corps History Division, 2014), 12; and Asselin, *Vietnam's American War*, 103–6.

Shufly Relief in Place

Shufly helicopter units operated on four-month rotations. Lieutenant Colonel Robert L. Rathbun's HMM-163 arrived at Soc Trang on 23 July 1962 to replace HMM-362. Like many of his contemporaries, Lieutenant Colonel Rathbun had considerable experience across multiple aircraft, spending five years each in fighters, transports, and helicopters, making him well versed in all aspects of Marine aviation.[62] To assist Rathbun's unit in familiarizing itself with the area, Clapp's squadron provided a week of orientation flights and continued operating alongside its Shufly relief.[63]

HMM-163 completed the relief in place on 31 July. Archie's Angels exited the combat theater after three-and-a-half months of combat operations from Soc Trang. In that time, crews tallied 50 combat assaults, 4,439 sorties, and 5,262 hours of flight time without losing a single aircraft or suffering any casualties. HMM-362 re-formed at Marine Corps Air Station Santa Ana, but its officers and enlisted received new orders, transferring to other squadrons to become a cadre of combat-experienced pilots and crews. The unit left its 24 HUS-1 Seahorses in Vietnam, handing them over to the 217th RVNAF Helicopter Squadron. Much of the leadership of Shufly also changed when HMM-362 redeployed. Lieutenant Colonel Julius W. Ireland replaced Colonel Carey on 30 July. Ireland was not new to Da Nang, having commanded Marine Attack Squadron 324 (VMA-324) in April 1954 during the French Indochina War.[64]

In their first month in the combat theater, "Rathbun's Ridgerunners" compiled a new Marine squadron record in Vietnam, flying 2,500 hours. Despite the monsoon season, they "worked 'round the clock, seven days a week," according to Lieutenant James R. Griffin. "While we were not in the air we were busy with maintenance on our aircraft, attending briefings, or trying to get a few hours [*sic*] sleep," he reported.[65] They adopted many of the tactics and techniques of their predecessor unit, but they rejected some established ones if deemed necessary. Combat experience taught crews that the earlier decision to rely on only M3A1 submachine guns or M1 Garand rifles for defensive fire was unsound. Following an evaluation of a mounted M-60 belt-fed machine gun to suppress light enemy ground fire, Rathbun authorized equipping all HUS-1s with the weapons inside the cargo hatches, a significant increase in firepower that gave crew chiefs a means of self-defense.[66] Strict USMACV rules of engagement applied, however, and crews could engage targets only after first receiving fire and clearly identifying enemy combatants.[67]

Shufly Moves North

On 16 September, Shufly began the Marine Corps' long association with the Republic of Vietnam's northern provinces. The squadron made a 10-hour, 617-kilometer movement to Da Nang, in Quang Nam Province, leaving the rice paddies of III Corps for the mountains and coastal plains of I Corps.[68] "Mobility is our business," one staff officer wryly quipped on the relocation.[69] HMM-163 swapped areas of operations with the U.S. Army's 93d Transportation Company (Light Helicopter), which had operated from Da Nang since February. Practicality dictated the substitution: the Army's anemic CH-21 Shawnees struggled in the rugged I Corps, while the more powerful Marine HUS-1 Seahorses were better suited to operating in the mountains.[70]

As the only deepwater port and anchorage in the region, Da Nang was a busy economic center. It had a commercial airport, seaplane service, rail line, and a well-maintained coastal road that connected it to the rest of the country. The architecture revealed its French naval base and resort town past. Da Nang's modern infrastructure included electricity, telephone

---

62 Richard Tregaskis, *Vietnam Diary* (New York: Holt, Rinehart, and Winston, 1963), 44.

63 Whitlow, *The Advisory and Combat Assistance Era, 1954–1964*, 70.

64 The unit delivered 25 Vought F4U Corsair fighters to the French Far East Expeditionary Corps as support aircraft in the Battle of Dien Bien Phu (1954), where Communist forces eventually surrounded and defeated the French. Whitlow, *The Advisory and Combat Assistance Era, 1954–1964*, 70–71.

65 As quoted in Spec5 Joe Groner, "Marine Copter Unit Leaves Vietnam," *Stars and Stripes Pacific Edition*, 23 January 1963.

66 Headquarters, Task Element 79.3.3.6, Marine Aircraft Group 16 (MAG-16), 1st MAW, "Evaluation of Helicopter Tactics and Techniques Report," 10 January 1963, attached to Headquarters, Task Element 79.3.3.6, MAG-16, 1st MAW Command Diary, 6 November 1962–28 January 1963, folder 61, U.S. Marine Corps History Division Vietnam War Documents Collection, item no. 1201061142, TTU Vietnam Archive, 7.

67 Whitlow, *The Advisory and Combat Assistance Era, 1954–1964*, 70.

68 Norman Sklarewitz, "Dateline Da Nang: The Choppers Move North," *Marine Corps Gazette* 47, no. 1 (January 1963): 3.

69 Sklarewitz, "Dateline Da Nang," 3.

70 Tregaskis, *Vietnam Diary*, 15; and "Battalion History, 93rd Transportation Company/121st AHC Early History," box 1, folder 8, VHPA Collection, item no 3110108001, TTU Vietnam Archive.

SHUFLY RELOCATION TO DA NANG, SEPTEMBER 1962

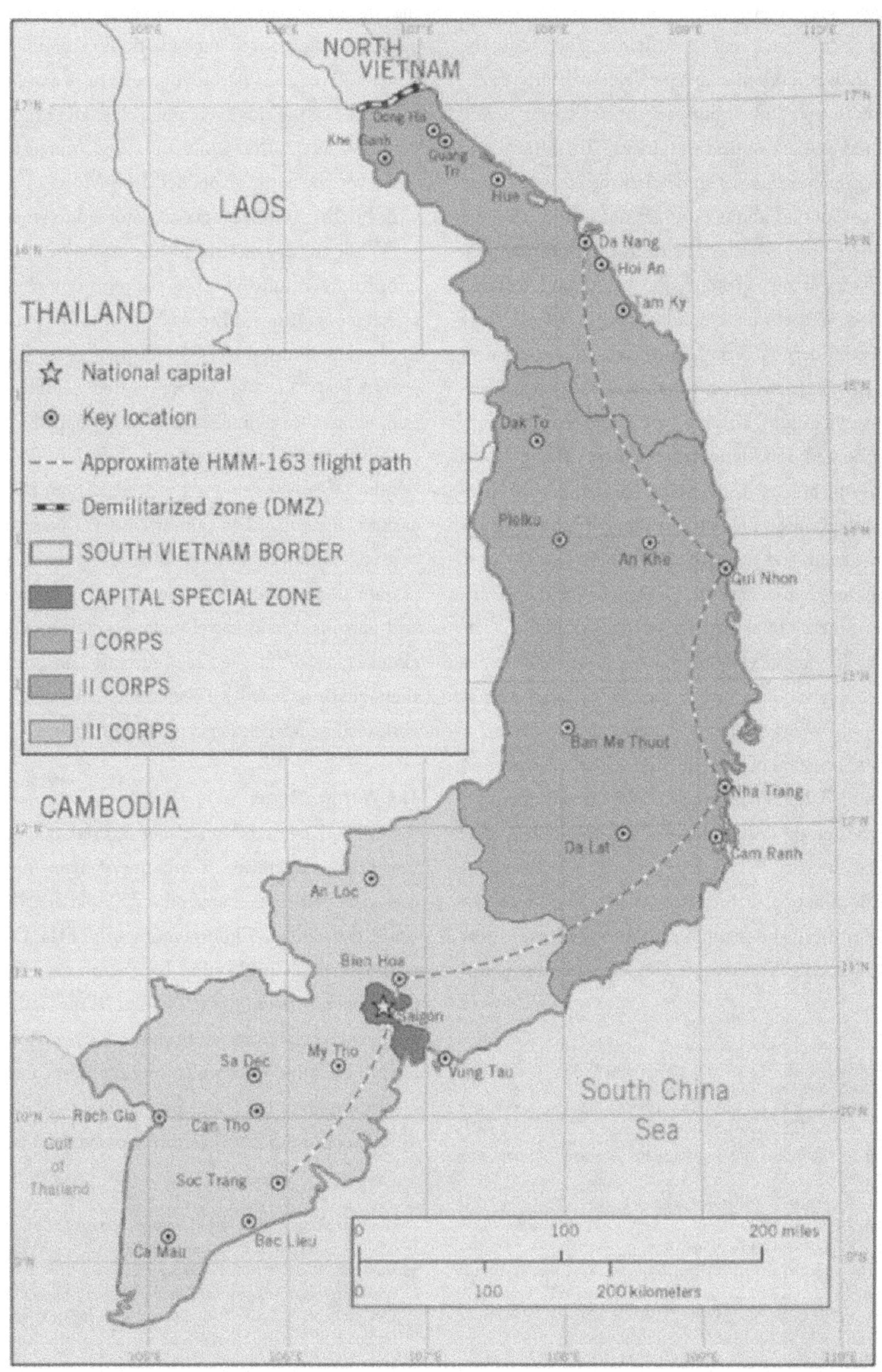

Map courtesy of Pete McPhail, adapted by MCUP

service, paved streets, and a developed waterfront, making the city of 100,000 a vibrant hub and a mix of European and Vietnamese character and culture.[71]

Compared to the small, remote airfield at Soc Trang, the Da Nang facility was modern and expansive. Its nearly three-kilometer runway and fully equipped control tower meant the airfield could operate around the clock.[72] The Shufly barracks area was "a picturesque, if somewhat run-down, former French army compound about one kilometer from the airstrip," remembered one Marine. Far from the primitive tent city scratched out of the Mekong, the compound featured numerous faded, yellow stucco buildings with red tile roofs alongside more modern facilities. Shufly Marines could now wash their laundry regularly, visit a dentist, attend chapel services, relax in service clubs, watch a movie, and see a barber.[73]

I Corps stretched 350 kilometers from the demilitarized zone (DMZ)—the border area between the Republic of Vietnam and Democratic Republic of Vietnam—to the II Corps boundary to the south and averaged 70 kilometers east to west. Its 16,000 square kilometers made I Corps larger than Connecticut and one-sixth of the total size of the Republic of Vietnam.[74] Each of its provinces bordered the South China Sea to the east. I Corps was also one of the RVN's most densely populated regions, with roughly 90 percent of its people living within 25 kilometers of the coastline. Quang Nam Province alone averaged 2,000 people per 1.5-square kilometers.[75] By contrast, the remote inland jungles and mountains were nearly devoid of civilians.[76]

The most dominating features around Da Nang were the abrupt transition from the piedmont to imposing peaks that rise to higher than 1,500 meters.[77] Heavily forested mountains with triple canopy in some places obscured any view of the ground. HMM-163 crews came to know that the line of mountains formed a barrier, trapping fog and rain and limiting air operations. Poor flying conditions on one side of the mountain could require instrument flight rules conditions while the other side of the ridge remained clear and bright. For helicopter crews, adaptation was mandatory. "You just grow into that wherever you're at," explained Bob Mills, a young lieutenant with HMM-163. "You get accustomed to what's going on."[78]

While the dry months mostly created water shortage problems for the Shufly Marines, the monsoon season's challenges affected operations.[79] From October to March, the flight ceiling became limited to 300–450 meters for days or weeks at a time. Fog, rain, and drizzle limited visibility to one or two kilometers. Occasionally, the ceiling dropped to 60 meters and visibility reduced to less than a kilometer.[80] Whereas the delta's flat landscape lessened concerns about flying overloaded aircraft, the rugged terrain around Da Nang required thorough operational planning. With so few suitable landing spots, pilots had to calculate fuel loads and usage, weight of cargo and personnel, and travel distances.[81] The constant rain and cloud cover often grounded aircraft and confined crews to their quarters, leaving Lieutenant Colonel Rathbun to deal with restless Marines and morale problems.[82]

The War in I Corps

As in the Mekong, Viet Cong fighters operated in Shufly's new area of operation, a mixture of main force and provincial units that totaled around 4,750 soldiers.[83] The task force's home was only 135 kilometers south of the DMZ, a hotspot of cross-border infiltration by Communist fighters. Hanoi's continual expansion of the Ho Chi Minh Trail, the network of roads and paths from north to south by way of the nominally neutral Laos and Cambodia, kept the Viet Cong well supplied.

Throughout 1961 and into early 1962, between 500 and 1,000 Communist infiltrators crossed into the Republic of

---

71 *U.S. Army Area Handbook for Vietnam*, 38, 51; and Whitlow, *The Advisory and Combat Assistance Era, 1954–1964*, 75.

72 Samuel Baez, "Vietnam's First Operational U.S. Marine Corps Deaths," *Leatherneck* 75, no. 11 (November 1992): 90.

73 David H. Hugel, "The Vietnam War: Shufly Remembered," *Leatherneck* 79, no. 4 (April 1996): 29.

74 Whitlow, *The Advisory and Combat Assistance Era, 1954–1964*, 78.

75 *U.S. Army Area Handbook for Vietnam*, 38, 51; and Whitlow, *The Advisory and Combat Assistance Era, 1954–1964*, 78.

76 Speech by Gen Lewis M. Walt to the Albuquerque Rotary Club, 21 August 1969, box 17, folder 7, Gen Keith B. McCutcheon Papers, HD Archive, 3.

77 Fails, *Marines and Helicopters, 1962–1973*, 79; Whitlow, *The Advisory and Combat Assistance Era, 1954–1964*, 78; and LtGen Keith B. McCutcheon, USMC, "Marine Aviation in Vietnam, 1962–1970," U.S. Naval Institute *Proceedings* 97, no. 5 (May 1971): 165.

78 Maj Bob Mills, USMC (Ret), interview with Kelly Crager, 4 May 2011, Bob Mills Collection, item no. OH0829, TTU Vietnam Archive, quote appears ca. 1:05:00 on audio recording.

79 Whitlow, *The Advisory and Combat Assistance Era, 1954–1964*, 112.

80 McCutcheon, "Marine Aviation in Vietnam," 165.

81 Tregaskis, *Vietnam Diary*, 62–63.

82 Tregaskis, *Vietnam Diary*, 61–62.

83 Whitlow, *The Advisory and Combat Assistance Era, 1954–1964*, 80.

I CORPS TACTICAL ZONE

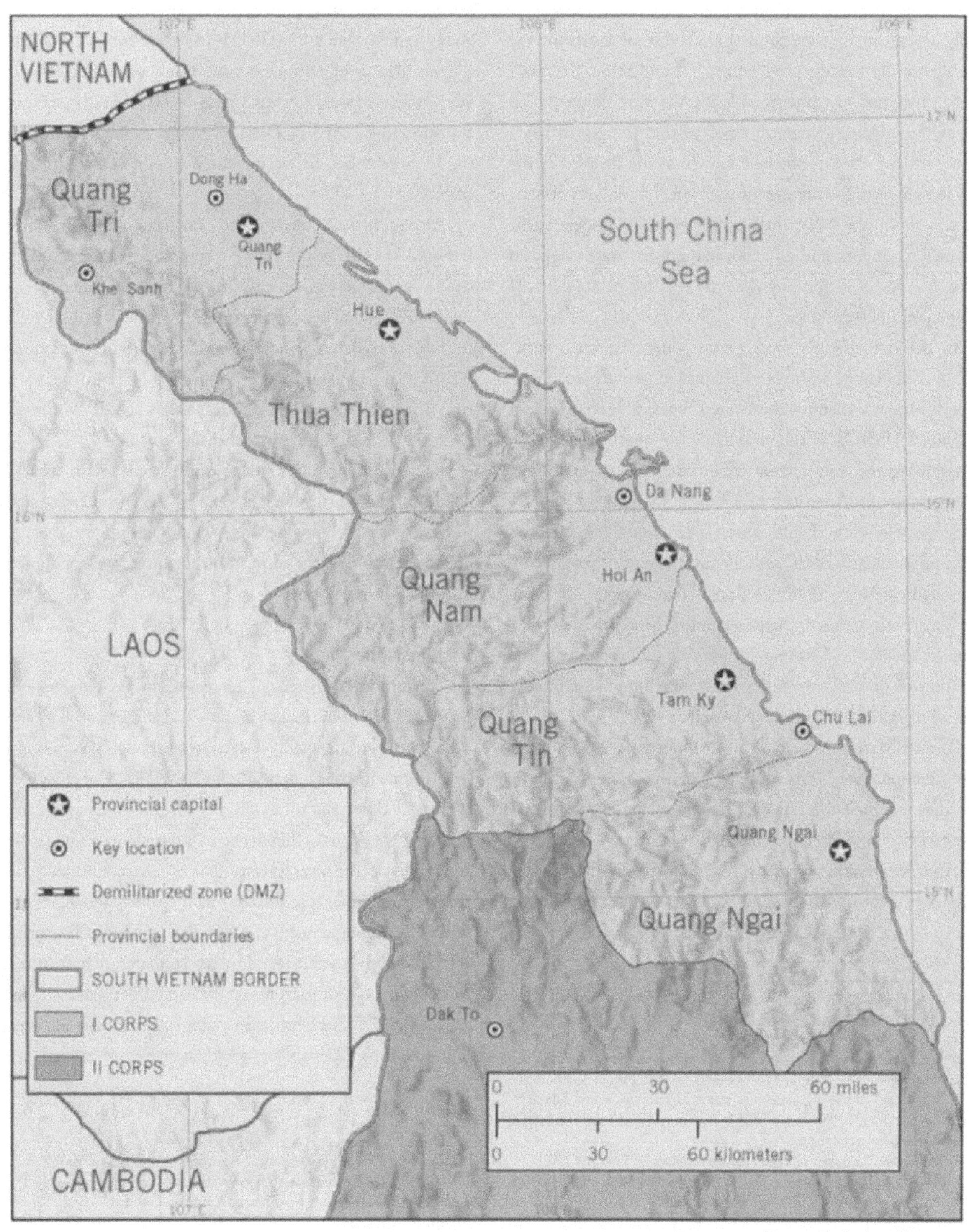

Map courtesy of Pete McPhail, adapted by MCUP

Vietnam from the north each month. They had undergone intensive political indoctrination and military training before making the trek and constituted a formidable force. Ideologically ardent, many were loyal to the cause of overthrowing the South Vietnamese government.[84] In addition, the Shufly Marines had to contend with the threat of conventional forces. American intelligence reported that the North Vietnamese Army (NVA), officially known as the People's Army of Vietnam, was positioning units on the border.[85] As of September 1962, one NVA infantry division, two independent infantry regiments, and an artillery regiment were staged in Laos, poised for action anywhere in I Corps or northern II Corps within 20 days.[86]

In the face of the growing insurgency, American military and civilian policy makers attempted to craft a comprehensive strategic plan for the United States to leave Vietnam by 1965.[87] USMACV aimed to assist the South Vietnamese in acquiring the long-term capability to defeat Communist threats after the American exit. South Vietnamese military forces grew in strength and means as additional U.S. advisors and equipment arrived throughout 1962. The principal strategy remained clearing and holding populated areas and denying the Viet Cong access to the population. The expanding influence in I Corps as Communist fighters infiltrated from the north made offensive operations in the mountains next to the coastal plains militarily advisable by late 1962.[88]

The 1st Marine Aircraft Wing's supporting role in I Corps was functionally no different than in the Mekong. Shufly Marines assumed the task of flying missions for an assortment of South Vietnamese forces, among them the 1st and 2d ARVN Divisions, elements of the 25th ARVN Division, ARVN Ranger battalions, and paramilitary units of varying sizes along the coastal plain.[89] ARVN ground commanders' previous experience working with the U.S. Army's 93d Transportation Company allowed for a quick transition between Army and Marine units. HMM-163's first combat mission in its new area of operations occurred only one day after all its aircraft arrived in Da Nang. Using 14 HUS-1s, the squadron transported 2d ARVN Division troops 55 kilometers south on 18 September, delivering them unopposed in steep hill country.[90]

Although their role was the same, the unfamiliar terrain required HMM-163 to refine tactics and techniques as they determined what worked best. The squadron modified its landing zone preparation, relying on both artillery and air strikes to clear prospective sites. The Marines also staged portable refueling bladders at secure locations to extend the squadron's operational reach.[91] As in the Mekong, ARVN forces in I Corps created heliborne fast reaction teams. In case of an emergency, infantry units were ready to deploy in what the Marines referred to as "Tiger Flights." As with Eagle Flights in the Mekong, the tactic was generally useful as a means to quickly reinforce isolated positions or insert a blocking force during offensive operations.[92]

First Casualties

As the tempo of operations increased for HMM-163—the only Marine unit in combat in the world at the time—its crews experienced steady enemy resistance. Although the amount of small-arms fire that the squadron received in I Corps was similar to the delta, the mountainous terrain forced pilots to fly predictably at times. They navigated passes in the mountains and landed in the few clearings that could accommodate their aircraft, sometimes into the teeth of prepared enemy gun positions. The consequence was a growing number of hits on aircraft and crew casualties.[93] HMM-163 aircraft first suffered battle damage near Tam Ky on 26 September while supporting the 2d ARVN Division. In a near full-squadron lift, one of the squadron's 22 Seahorses took damage from enemy small-

[84] Graham A. Cosmas, *MACV: The Joint Command in the Years of Escalation, 1962–1967* (Washington, DC: Center of Military History, United States Army, 2006), 73–74.

[85] American personnel used the term *North Vietnamese Army* (NVA) when discussing regular forces from the Democratic Republic of Vietnam. In keeping with this tradition, this book will primarily use NVA, substituting People's Army of Vietnam where it is appropriate to use the official title, such as in unit names.

[86] Whitlow, *The Advisory and Combat Assistance Era, 1954–1964*, 80.

[87] Kaplan, Landa, and Drea, *The McNamara Ascendancy, 1961–1965*, 281–82; and Cosmas, *MACV: The Joint Command in the Years of Escalation, 1962–1967*, 75–86.

[88] Whitlow, *The Advisory and Combat Assistance Era, 1954–1964*, 80.

[89] Whitlow, *The Advisory and Combat Assistance Era, 1954–1964*, 79.

[90] Whitlow, *The Advisory and Combat Assistance Era, 1954–1964*, 80.

[91] Whitlow, *The Advisory and Combat Assistance Era, 1954–1964*, 82.

[92] Whitlow, *The Advisory and Combat Assistance Era, 1954–1964*, 82–84.

[93] Sklarewitz, "Dateline Da Nang," 3.

Archie J. Clapp Collection, Archives Branch, Marine Corps History Division

HMM-362 supporting ARVN troops in 1962.

arms fire. Another four aircraft were hit during the following week, killing two ARVN soldiers and wounding a crew chief.[94]

The first Shufly Marines killed in action in Vietnam were lost in early October 1962. Lieutenant Colonel Rathbun's squadron received a request for 20 helicopters to lift elements of the 2d ARVN Division. On 6 October, HUS-1 BuNo 145790 flew as the search and rescue aircraft on the mission, 1 of 20 aircraft involved in the strike. On board were eight men: the helicopter commander, copilot, crew chief/gunner, two Navy medical personnel, and three mechanics to repair and rescue any helicopters that were forced down. Flying in formation with the sea to their portside and the mountainous terrain to their starboard, the aircraft experienced mechanical problems. Breaking off from the flight, aircraft commander First Lieutenant William T. Sinnott turned his UH-34 inland to make the 80-kilometer return trip to Da Nang. Fifteen kilometers off the coast where the coastal plain transitioned into mountainous jungle, the helicopter flew into a valley choked with dense gray cumulus clouds. Vertigo disoriented Sinnott and the aircraft crashed into a thickly forested ridge.[95]

The Seahorse caught fire on impact and rapidly reduced to ash. Seven men died in the crash or in the ensuing hours: First Lieutenant Michael J. Tunney, Sergeant Herald W. Pen-

[94] Whitlow, *The Advisory and Combat Assistance Era, 1954–1964*, 80.

[95] Tregaskis, *Vietnam Diary*, 23; and Baez, "Vietnam's First Operational U.S. Marine Corps Deaths," 90–91.

dell, Corporal Thomas E. Anderson, Lieutenant (MC) Gerald C. Griffin, Sergeant Richard E. Hamilton, Lance Corporal Miguel A. Valentin Jr., and Hospital Corpsman Second Class Gerald O. Norton.[96] Despite the best efforts of Marine and ARVN rescuers, the thick jungle made quick extraction impossible. They methodically descended the hill with the injured in search of a clearing for a landing zone. The sun set as the litter parties made slow progress. By the next morning, Lieutenant Sinnott was the sole survivor from the crash. Around 0700, Lieutenant Colonel Rathbun arrived overhead piloting an HUS and rushed Sinnott nearly 500 kilometers down the coast to the U.S. Army 8th Field Hospital at Nha Trang.[97] The circumstances leading to the crash became familiar hazards to countless Marine helicopter crews who operated in I Corps' rugged terrain and unpredictable weather.

Transitioning Fixed-Wing Pilots to Helicopters

Combat operations in Vietnam demanded that the Marine Corps continually funnel personnel and machines toward the expanding helicopter program, which included as many as 13 squadrons by mid-1962. The scheduled rotation of squadrons in Vietnam, and the increasing usefulness of helicopters operating from the new landing platform helicopter (LPH) ships off the coast in the South China Sea, strained resources. By summer 1962, the number of helicopter pilots the Marine Corps required was 40 percent of the Service's overall aviator pool, around 1,200 personnel. However, only 29 percent of Marine aviators were available to fly rotary-wing aircraft.[98] The high demand for rotary-wing pilots affected personal lives and careers, as near constant deployments kept Marines from their home stations. Exhausted by the commitments and looking for opportunities elsewhere, a growing number of rated helicopter pilots left the Service, worsening the problem.[99]

In November 1962, the Marine Corps reassigned 500 fixed-wing aviators who had at least one operational tour to helicopters. Planners predicted that the retraining program would provide about 86 percent of the required rotary-wing pilots by June 1964 and fill the need for more first lieutenants and captains.[100] Between 100 and 125 pilots were to transition each year and be assigned to two squadrons, one on each U.S. coast. The aviators would spend 46 hours in the classroom and another 65 hours in flight training in the UH-34D Seahorse, earning them copilot status.[101]

The retraining took place at Marine Corps Air Facility Santa Ana and Marine Corps Air Station Cherry Point, North Carolina. HMM-362, the first Shufly squadron, reorganized as a training squadron at Santa Ana and began preparing the first pilots to transition to rotary-wing aircraft in November. The following month, HMM-262 similarly reconstituted as a training squadron and instructed pilots at Cherry Point. For almost two years, 10 fixed-wing pilots joined each helicopter squadron every month.[102] Many of the original Archie's Angels served as instructors in both training squadrons, imparting lessons from Vietnam. The Marine Corps' infusion of talent into helicopter squadrons and use of a combat veteran unit as a training cadre prepared Marine rotary-wing aviation for the increasing commitment in Southeast Asia in the coming years.[103]

Extending Shufly

In late 1962, the 1st MAW extended tours in Vietnam for helicopter squadrons and supporting units to six months—two more than originally planned.[104] The extension was 1st MAW's attempt to introduce continuity and use manpower more effectively in Vietnam. On 11 January 1963, the "Dough Boys" of HMM-162 relieved HMM-163. During its tour, Lieutenant Colonel Rathbun's squadron flew nearly 11,000 hours, conducted 15,200 sorties, and transported 23,200 assault troops.[105]

---

96 Baez, "Vietnam's First Operational US Marine Corps Deaths," 90–91; and Tregaskis, *Vietnam Diary*, 16.

97 Tregaskis, *Vietnam Diary*, 19–20; Whitlow, *The Advisory and Combat Assistance Era, 1954–1964*, 83; Lt Gerald Charles Griffin, USN, U.S. Navy Veterans Online Memorial, accessed 21 February 2020; and "KIA Incident 19621006, HMM-163, UH-34D, 145790+—Mechanical Failure," USMC Combat and Tiltrotor Association, accessed 21 February 2020.

98 Fails, *Marines and Helicopters, 1962–1973*, 69.

99 "500 Pilots to Retrain for Helicopter Duty," *Marine Corps Gazette* 46, no. 10 (October 1962): 1.

100 Fails, *Marines and Helicopters, 1962–1973*, 70.

101 "500 Pilots to Retrain for Helicopter Duty," 1.

102 Fails, *Marines and Helicopters, 1962–1973*, 70.

103 Fails, *Marines and Helicopters, 1962–1973*, 69–70.

104 Whitlow, *The Advisory and Combat Assistance Era, 1954–1964*, 83; and Fails, *Marines and Helicopters, 1962–1973*, 80.

105 Weekly Summary [1st MAW], 6–12 January 1963, folder 67, U.S. Marine Corps History Division Vietnam War Documents Collection, item no. 1201067185, TTU Vietnam Archive, 2.

Lieutenant Colonel Reinhardt Leu, another veteran aviator, commanded HMM-162. His unit conducted its first major combat assault a week after arriving, supporting the 2d ARVN Division 25 kilometers west of Da Nang. Eighteen UH-34Ds airlifted 300 ARVN troops into three landing zones to sweep a suspected Viet Cong base area. Poor weather conditions in I Corps persisted for the next three months, restricting flight operations to logistical sorties rather than tactical support missions.[106]

The fast pace of combat missions resumed as better flying weather returned in April. The quicker operational tempo also meant higher losses. HMM-162 conducted a major assault on 13 April, lifting 435 soldiers from the 2d ARVN Division against another Viet Cong base area in the mountains 50 kilometers south of Da Nang. The mission was the first instance in the war of armed helicopters rather than fixed-wing aircraft escorting Marine UH-34s, as five U.S. Army UH-1B Iroquois gunships from the Da Nang-based 68th Aviation Company launched preparatory strikes against the landing zones.[107]

The first insertions were unopposed. In late afternoon, First Lieutenant Stephen W. Pless's UH-34 was ordered to evacuate three casualties. The aircraft took small arms fire on approach, but the fire ceased while the helicopter was on the ground loading the personnel. On takeoff, a burst of .50-caliber machine gun fire raked the cockpit, wounding the copilot. About 20 rounds in total damaged the helicopter, enough to force it down.[108] Pless explained in his report that there was "confusion as usual. Then shots were heard and we went down in our crippled bird."[109] When two HMM-162 helicopters arrived to evacuate the crew and seven passengers, enemy fire forced down one of the Seahorses near Pless's aircraft and badly wounded the crew chief, Corporal Charley M. Campbell. An accompanying helicopter rushed him to Da Nang for treatment. Five kilometers away, another UH-34D supporting the same operation went down after taking hits on final approach. Its crew made a quick field repair and limped the aircraft back to Da Nang.[110]

[106] Whitlow, *The Advisory and Combat Assistance Era, 1954–1964*, 113.
[107] Whitlow, *The Advisory and Combat Assistance Era, 1954–1964*, 115.
[108] Remarks attached to After Action Report, Marine Task Unit 79.3.3.6, Mission Order Number 4-169-2, 13 April 1962, HD Archive.
[109] Remarks attached to After Action Report, Marine Task Unit 79.3.3.6.
[110] Whitlow, *The Advisory and Combat Assistance Era, 1954–1964*, 115.

Two weeks later, the Shufly Marines observed that "tension" was increasing "in the Da Nang area due to indications of [Viet Cong] activity nearby."[111] Likewise, beginning in late April, tension increased near the Laotian border. HMM-162 was central to the South Vietnamese response. Over 90 days, the squadron supported a 1st ARVN Division offensive in the rugged mountains of Quang Tri and Thua Thien Provinces, denying the Communists infiltration routes near the border and sweeping suspected base areas.[112]

Lieutenant Colonel Leu's HMM-162 completed its six-month deployment on 8 June 1963.[113] After nearly 17,700 sorties, it lost only three helicopters.[114] Their relief squadron was the New River-based "Bulls" of HMM-261 under the command of Lieutenant Colonel Frank A. Shook, another veteran helicopter pilot with combat experience in the Korean War. HMM-261 flew its first missions the same day it relieved HMM-162. Due to enemy action in the village of Phuoc Lam, the Bulls evacuated Vietnamese women and children to Da Nang.[115]

HMM-261 refined Shufly's tactics during its deployment, much of it regarding the protection of aircraft from enemy ground fire. It standardized helicopters flying at a minimum of 450 meters during missions. Flight leaders now conducted visual reconnaissance before entering landing zones. Given that all Shufly squadrons experienced the bulk of aircraft damage while in landing zones, HMM-261 recommended

[111] Weekly Summary [1st MAW], 21–27 April 1963, folder 67, U.S. Marine Corps History Division Vietnam War Documents Collection, item no. 1201067185, TTU Vietnam Archive, 2.
[112] Whitlow, *The Advisory and Combat Assistance Era, 1954–1964*, 115; and Weekly Summary [1st MAW], 26 May–1 June 1963, folder 67, U.S. Marine Corps History Division Vietnam War Documents Collection, item no. 1201067185, TTU Vietnam Archive, 2.
[113] Command Diary, Headquarters, Task Element 79.3.3.6, MAG-16, 1st MAW, 1 May 1963–17 July 1963, folder 62, U.S. Marine Corps History Division Vietnam War Documents Collection, item no. 1201062005, TTU Vietnam Archive, 10.
[114] Whitlow, *The Advisory and Combat Assistance Era, 1954–1964*, 116.
[115] Weekly Summary [1st MAW], 9–15 June 1963, folder 67, U.S. Marine Corps History Division Vietnam War Documents Collection, item no. 1201067185, TTU Vietnam Archive; and Command Diary, Headquarters, Task Element 79.3.3.6, MAG-16, 1st MAW, 1 May 1963–17 July 1963, 10.

Bell UH-1 "Huey"

Defense Department (Marine Corps), photo by LCpl Alex Wasinski

In February 1954, the U.S. Army announced a design competition for its first turbine-powered helicopter. Based on experience from the Korean War, it desired a relatively light and powerful utility helicopter. Bell Helicopter won the competition with the H-40, powered by the new Lycoming T53 turboshaft powerplant, leading to a design contract in June 1955. The first production model, the HU-1A Iroquois, arrived in July 1959 and the upgraded HU-1B in April 1961. As part of the November 1962 Department of Defense redesignations, the Iroquois became the UH-1. However, the HU-1 designation had already given the aircraft its popular nickname: the "Huey."

Bell UH-1s first deployed to the Republic of Vietnam in April 1962 as medical evacuation (medevac/dustoff) aircraft with the Army's 57th Medical Detachment. Armed variants began operations in October 1962. Updated UH-1Bs arrived later in the year fitted with the first professionally engineered external armament kits for a helicopter, including the Emerson Electric M-6E3 flexible quad-machine gun system equipped with four 7.62mm M60s (two on either side of the fuselage), and 14 2.75-inch folding-fin aerial rockets.

In 1962, the Marine Corps chose the UH-1 to replace the Kaman HH-43 Huskie observation helicopter. Its variant of the Huey was designated the UH-1E—the Marines did not share the Army's custom of naming its helicopters after Native American tribes. The UH-1E was identical to the UH-1B in terms of airframe design, Lycoming T53-1-11 powerplant, and rotor system, but it differed in some aspects in order to meet the requirements of an amphibious force. While Army variants used lightweight magnesium components, the material's propensity to corrode when exposed to salt water, and its dangerous volatility upon catching fire, forced the replacement of many parts with aluminum. The UH-1Es were also fitted with specific radios, avionics, and revised electrical systems, as well as brakes to stop spinning rotors quickly and keep them stationary when on board ship. The initial delivery of a handful of UH-1Es occurred in October 1963. Production versions began arriving in February 1964. The Marines sent the first armed versions to Vietnam in 1965 and ultimately received 208 aircraft by the end of the production run in September 1968.[1]

[1] "Army Planning New Helicopter Designs," *Aviation Week* 58, no. 16 (20 April 1953): 21; "Bell HU-1A Helicopter Ordered in Production," *Aviation Week* 68, no. 7 (17 February 1958): 34; and Bill Siuru, *The Huey and Huey Cobra* (Blue Ridge Summit, PA: TAB Books, 1987), 71–80.

Archie J. Clapp Collection, Archives Branch, Marine Corps History Division

An HMM-362 aircraft supporting ARVN troops.

coordinated close air support from T-28s Trojans and AD-6 Skyraiders during casualty evacuation sorties.[116]

HMM-261 redeployed to New River on 30 September. The squadron flew 11,400 sorties, clocked nearly 5,300 hours in combat, lifted more than 6,000 troops and almost 2 million pounds of cargo, and conducted more than 600 casualty evacuations.[117] HMM-261 transferred authority of Shufly operations on 2 October 1963 to the "Flying Tigers" of HMM-361 led by Lieutenant Colonel Thomas J. Ross, a decorated fighter pilot in World War II and the Korean War.[118]

In its first month, HMM-361 experienced more enemy encounters in a four-week period than any Shufly squadron to that point, taking fire on 46 different occasions.[119] The squadron's first casualties occurred on 8 October when two of its

[116] Headquarters, Task Element 79.3.3.6, MAG-16, 1st MAW, "Evaluation of Helicopter Tactics and Techniques Report," 19 July 1963, attached to Headquarters, Task Element 79.3.3.6, MAG-16, 1st MAW Command Diary, 1 May 1963–17 July 1963, folder 62, U.S. Marine Corps History Division Vietnam War Documents Collection, item no. 1201062005, TTU Vietnam Archive, 2.

[117] Whitlow, *The Advisory and Combat Assistance Era, 1954–1964*, 117–20.

[118] Weekly Summary [1st MAW], 28 September–4 October 1963, folder 67, U.S. Marine Corps History Division Vietnam War Documents Collection, item no. 1201067185, TTU Vietnam Archive, 2; and Biography of Thomas J. Ross.

[119] Weekly Summary [1st MAW], 28 September–4 October 1963, 2; Weekly Summary [1st MAW], 5–11 October 1963, 2; Weekly Summary [1st MAW], 12–18 October 1963, 2; Weekly Summary [1st MAW], 19–25 October 1963, 2; and Weekly Summary [1st MAW], 26 October–1 November 1963, 2. All found in folder 67, U.S. Marine Corps History Division Vietnam War Documents Collection, item no. 1201067185, TTU Vietnam Archive.

UH-34Ds crashed while responding to a downed RVNAF T-28 some 65 kilometers southwest of Da Nang. Fading light halted the recovery operation. The next day, a recovery team found the bodies of the pilots and copilots, HMM-361's flight surgeon, and five crew among the wreckage. Evidence of bullet damage made clear that the enemy scored hits on the aircraft while in flight. Due to the close proximity of the wrecks, however, the recovery team could not rule out a midair collision.[120]

USMACV planned to withdraw more than 1,000 Americans from Vietnam by the end of 1963, including the Shufly Marines at Da Nang. However, the Marine Corps extended Shufly operations until the first half of 1964 to train RVNAF pilots and crews to fly UH-34s. Upon completion, the Marines would transfer their aircraft to the RVNAF and end Shufly operations. On 22 January 1964, the Joint Chiefs of Staff approved the Marine Corps' 30 June deadline for the training and aircraft handover.[121] The "Purple Foxes" of HMM-364 assumed the additional task, beginning operations at Da Nang on 1 February. The new program provided crucial training backed by experience. As a result, commanding general of Fleet Marine Force, Pacific, Lieutenant General Victor H. Krulak, requested and received approval from the Joint Chiefs to maintain the task force and postpone the rotation of Marine helicopter squadrons. Shufly would continue to operate as the American involvement in Vietnam expanded.[122]

Deepening U.S. Military Commitment

A series of political events involving the South Vietnamese government contributed to the extension of Marine rotary-wing operations in Vietnam. On 2 October 1963, Secretary of Defense Robert S. McNamara and General Taylor, now Chairman of the Joint Chiefs of Staff, submitted a report to President Kennedy on the military situation in the Republic of Vietnam. They concluded that victory was possible, but it would require a continuation of the U.S. military advisory effort until 1965.[123]

On 1 November, a group of ARVN officers overthrew the South Vietnamese government and killed President Ngo Dinh Diem.[124] The instability evidenced by the coup prompted a renewed American commitment in Vietnam to stabilize the political and military situation. Three weeks later, President Kennedy was assassinated in Dallas, Texas. Vice President Lyndon B. Johnson inherited a steadily growing American commitment in Southeast Asia. His approach was not dissimilar to Kennedy's, as he chose gradual escalation of U.S. military intervention rather than wholesale commitment from the outset.[125] On 7 February 1964, Communist fighters launched a wave of attacks across Vietnam, the largest against the U.S. compound and airfield at Pleiku in the Central Highlands. At the urging of many of his advisors, who called for swift retribution, President Johnson authorized limited retaliatory air strikes against DRV targets. The United States and the South Vietnamese governments claimed that these were justified, as they were direct responses to the ongoing Hanoi-organized infiltrations into the south and Viet Cong attacks. In an address to the nation, President Johnson made clear his conviction to support the Republic of Vietnam and help guarantee its security and independence.[126]

For Shufly, little changed during the first half of 1964. The end of the planned withdrawal at the close of 1963 and finite extension for training purposes had made it appear the task force was at an end. In May, USMACV ordered HMM-364 to transfer their aircraft to the 217th RVNAF Squadron. The rotation of Shufly units continued uninterrupted when HMM-162 returned to South Vietnam on 17 June, the first Marine helicopter squadron to redeploy for a second tour.[127] The U.S. posture toward the war began to change, however, following reported North Vietnamese attacks on the destroyer USS *Maddox* (DD 731) on 2 August 1964 in the Gulf of Tonkin off the coast of the Democratic Republic of Vietnam. The U.S. Congress passed the Gulf of Tonkin Resolution on 7 August, authorizing President Johnson to use conventional

---

120 Weekly Summary [1st MAW], 5–11 October 1963, 3; and Whitlow, *The Advisory and Combat Assistance Era, 1954–1964*, 120.

121 Fails, *Marines and Helicopters, 1962–1973*, 80.

122 Fails, *Marines and Helicopters, 1962–1973*, 80.

123 Kaplan, Landa, and Drea, *The McNamara Ascendancy*, 288–90.

124 Philip E. Catton, *Diem's Final Failure: Prelude to America's War in Vietnam* (Lawrence: University Press of Kansas, 2002), 200–2.

125 Fredrik Logevall, *Choosing War: The Lost Chance for Peace and the Escalation of War in Vietnam* (Berkeley: University of California Press, 1999).

126 Graham A. Cosmas, *The Joint Chiefs of Staff and the War in Vietnam, 1960–1968*, pt. 2 (Washington, DC: Office of Joint History, Office of the Chairman of the Joint Chiefs of Staff, 2012), 213–15.

127 See "Appendix: Marine Rotary-Wing Chronology during the Vietnam War."

military forces in Southeast Asia without a formal declaration of war.[128]

Shufly's existence to this point had been part of limited U.S. military support for the Republic of Vietnam. However, the escalation of the war and the greater American involvement necessitated changes to the organizational scheme of Marine helicopter support. Officially, the last task force squadron was Lieutenant Colonel Joseph Koler Jr.'s HMM-365, which replaced Lieutenant Colonel Oliver W. Curtis's HMM-162 in October 1964. On the final day of the calendar year, Fleet Marine Forces, Pacific, changed the designation of Marine helicopter operations from Task Element 79.3.3.6 to Task Unit 79.3.5, Marine Unit, Vietnam. Lieutenant Colonel Koler's HMM-365 remained in-country until Lieutenant Colonel Norman G. Ewers's HMM-163 relieved it on 17 February 1965 in a scheduled rotation as Marine Unit, Vietnam's operating squadron.[129] The name change did not alter the mission. Command and control relationships also remained the same, as USMACV had operational control over the task unit while the 1st MAW's commanding general retained responsibility for administrative and logistical support.[130]

The military and political situation in Vietnam in early 1965 had deteriorated to the extent that the White House concluded that the only policy options were to escalate or withdraw. Johnson believed that direct U.S. military involvement alone could prevent a collapse of the South Vietnamese government and a Communist victory in Southeast Asia.[131] In February, Army General William C. Westmoreland, who took command of USMACV the previous June, proposed deploying ground troops as security forces for major U.S. bases. On 20 February, the Joint Chiefs of Staff recommended to Secretary McNamara that a Marine expeditionary brigade (MEB) of about 8,500 officers and enlisted deploy to protect Da Nang Air Base. The commander in chief, United States Pacific Command, Admiral Ulysses S. Grant Sharp Jr., thought the situation in South Vietnam warranted sending a MEB to Da Nang, but phased in gradually.[132] He recommended first sending the command and control element, a helicopter squadron, and a battalion landing team. Existing Marine security forces at Da Nang could make up a second battalion landing team, and a third could be sent when there was adequate logistical support for it. The Joint Chiefs agreed with Sharp's plan and immediately forwarded it to McNamara.[133]

In response to escalating Communist attacks against American and South Vietnamese installations and a crumbling government in Saigon, on 26 February 1965 the Johnson administration approved deploying Marine units to Vietnam to protect the Da Nang Air Base.[134] Johnson authorized deploying a helicopter squadron and two battalion landing teams to Da Nang, and on 6 March he ordered 3,500 more Marines to Da Nang.[135]

On 8 March, the 9th Marine Expeditionary Brigade arrived at Da Nang. The brigade included two battalion landing teams: 3d Battalion, 9th Marines, and 1st Battalion, 3d Marines. As the buildup of forces continued, the 9th MEB took operational control of the Da Nang area with Brigadier General Frederick J. Karch in command.[136] The arrival of the first U.S. ground combat units marked the transition from providing the RVN with military assistance to an Americanization of the war.[137]

It also meant the resumption of the air-ground team concept around which Marine operations were based. Changes to the Marine Corps' aviation units in Vietnam accompanied the deployment of Marine ground combat units. The 9th Marine Expeditionary Brigade absorbed the helicopters of Marine Unit, Vietnam, making them an organic part of the air-ground team within the brigade. The headquarters of

[128] The Gulf of Tonkin Resolution or the Southeast Asia Resolution, Pub.L. 88–408, 78 Stat. 384, 10 August 1964; and Logevall, *Choosing War*, 324–26.

[129] *USMC/Vietnam Helicopter Association: Pop a Smoke*, 13; and Jack Shulimson and Maj Charles M. Johnson, USMC, *U.S. Marines in Vietnam: The Landing and the Buildup, 1965* (Washington, DC: History and Museums Division, Headquarters, U.S. Marine Corps, 1978), 235.

[130] Whitlow, *The Advisory and Combat Assistance Era, 1954–1964*, 165; and Shulimson and Johnson, *The Landing and the Buildup, 1965*, 235.

[131] Kaplan, Landa, and Drea, *The McNamara Ascendancy*, 532–33.

[132] Cosmas, *The Joint Chiefs of Staff and the War in Vietnam, 1960–1968*, pt. 2, 238–39.

[133] Cosmas, *The Joint Chiefs of Staff and the War in Vietnam, 1960–1968*, pt. 2, 239; and Kaplan, Landa, and Drea, *The McNamara Ascendancy*, 532–33.

[134] Kaplan, Landa, and Drea, *The McNamara Ascendancy*, 532; and Shulimson and Johnson, *The Landing and the Buildup, 1965*, 16.

[135] Edward J. Drea, *History of the Office of the Secretary of Defense*, vol. 6, *McNamara, Clifford, and the Burdens of Vietnam, 1965–1969* (Washington, DC: Historical Office, Office of the Secretary of Defense, 2011), 24.

[136] Col Rod Andrew Jr., USMCR, *The First Fight: U.S. Marines in Operation Starlite, August 1965*, Marines in the Vietnam War Commemorative Series (Quantico, VA: Marine Corps History Division, 2015), 3.

[137] Kaplan, Landa, and Drea, *The McNamara Ascendancy*, 532; and Shulimson and Johnson, *The Landing and the Buildup, 1965*, 15.

Defense Department (Marine Corps) A183773

UH-34D Bureau Number (BuNo) 150255 from HMM-162 lands among billowing dust on Hill 327 southwest of Da Nang on 10 March 1965.

Marine Aircraft Group 16 (MAG-16) moved from Okinawa to Da Nang beginning on 8 March. Colonel John H. King Jr., the overall commander of the short-lived successor to Shufly at the time, assumed command of the aircraft group.[138] MAG-16 included two medium helicopter squadrons: Lieutenant Colonel Norman Ewers's HMM-163 and Lieutenant Colonel Oliver Curtis's HMM-162.[139] In the midst of the changes, helicopter operations kept pace. The two squadrons flew more than 2,200 sorties by the end of March. Half occurred in a 13-square kilometer area around Da Nang, while the others supported ARVN ground operations throughout I Corps.[140]

In early April, 3d Battalion, 4th Marines, arrived in Vietnam and moved to Hue, 70 kilometers north of Da Nang. The unit required more responsive helicopter support than MAG-16 could provide from Da Nang, leading HMM-162 to establish a detachment of 10 UH-34Ds at the Phu Bai airstrip. Additional helicopter support trickled in during the ensuing weeks. Lieutenant Colonel George F. Bauman's VMO-2 arrived at Da Nang on 3 May. A detachment from VMO-2 had been part of Shufly since the initial deployment to Soc

[138] Fails, *Marines and Helicopters*, 92; and Shulimson and Johnson, *The Landing and the Buildup, 1965*, 18.

[139] Shulimson and Johnson, *The Landing and the Buildup, 1965*, 17.

[140] "1st Marine Aircraft Wing Operations, Vol. 1," folder 67, U.S. Marine Corps History Division Vietnam War Documents Collection, item no. 1201067181, TTU Vietnam Archive, 6-1.

Defense Department (Marine Corps)

Approaching Da Nang Air Base in 1965.

Trang in 1962. Now assigned to the 9th MEB, the remainder of the squadron relocated from Okinawa, bringing with it three Cessna O-1 Bird Dog liaison and observation aircraft.[141] Most importantly, it arrived with six armed Bell UH-1Es, the first helicopter gunships procured by the Marine Corps.[142]

After three years of operational isolation in Vietnam, Marine helicopters rejoined infantry units as part of the air-ground team that vertical envelopment doctrine prescribed. Helicopter operations were entering a new phase.[143] The war's escalation also brought a change in mission for the Marines. The 9th MEB was permitted to take part in "active combat" under conditions established by Secretary McNamara with the support of Secretary of State D. Dean Rusk. The Marines, therefore, could launch offensive operations to locate and engage enemy forces after 14 April.[144]

A New Phase for Marine Helicopters

When the first ground combat elements landed at Da Nang in March 1965, the Marine Corps had 20 helicopter squadrons spread around the globe. Fourteen were medium transport squadrons, 12 of which flew UH-34Ds. Three observation units flew a mixture of Cessna O-1 Bird Dogs, Kaman HOK-1

[141] The 1962 Tri-Service designation system changed the OE-1 to the O-1.

[142] Fails, *Marines and Helicopters, 1962–1973*, 81; and VMO-2 Command Chronology (ComdC), 29 April 1965–31 March 1966, folder 69, U.S. Marine Corps History Division Vietnam War Documents Collection, item no. 1201069086, TTU Vietnam Archive, 1.

[143] Shulimson and Johnson, *The Landing and the Buildup, 1965*, 15.

[144] Shulimson and Johnson, *The Landing and the Buildup, 1965*, 23.

Defense Department (Marine Corps) A184049

A squad from 1st Battalion, 3d Marines, rushes to a waiting UH-34D en route to joining a reconnaissance patrol east of Da Nang in April 1965.

(OH-43) Huskies, and Bell UH-1E "Huey" utility helicopters. Two squadrons still operated the aging Sikorsky CH-37C heavy-lift helicopter, and a final squadron was still forming.[145] Meanwhile, the Marine Corps was phasing in the tandem-rotor, twin-turbine Boeing-Vertol CH-46A Sea Knight. The CH-46 would eventually become the workhorse of Marine rotary-wing operations in Southeast Asia, as it could carry two to three times the number of troops as the UH-34D. For the time being, however, Marine operations in Vietnam still relied on the dependable UH-34s. At the start of the buildup in 1965, HMM-263 operated from the amphibious assault ship USS *Princeton* while HMM-162 and HMM-163 flew from Da Nang, along with a detachment of fixed-wing observation aircraft.[146]

From the start of Shufly in April 1962, a detachment of O-1E Bird Dogs from VMO-2 operated alongside the task group's medium helicopter squadron. Small airplanes mostly supplemented UH-1Es, which had taken over as the principal Marine observation aircraft from the O-1E and HOK-1 helicopter.[147] VMO-2 began using Hueys in the reconnaissance role as part of MAG-16 in May 1965 alongside the Cessnas. Flying out of Ky Ha, Marine Aircraft Group 36 (MAG-36) and its attached VMO-6 started operating in September 1965, giving the Marine Corps two observation squadrons within

[145] The 1962 Tri-Service aviation designation system changed the Marine Corps designation HR2S-1 to CH-37C.

[146] *USMC/Vietnam Helicopter Association: Pop a Smoke*, 79.

[147] LtCol Gary W. Parker, USMC, and Maj Frank M. Batha Jr., USMC, *A History of Marine Observation Squadron Six* (Washington, DC: History and Museums Division, Headquarters, U.S. Marine Corps, 1982), 35.

the 1st MAW in Vietnam. A third squadron, VMO-3, started operating out of Phu Bai in January 1967.[148]

VMO-2, -3, and -6 were equivalent in number to the entire prewar helicopter observation force. They flew UH-1Es exclusively, each operating from 21 to 27 aircraft.[149] The Huey filled dual roles in the VMO: observation and assault support. Ground forces and vulnerable transport helicopters required instantaneous suppression of enemy ground fire in landing zones. While many Marines would concede that fixed-wing support was superior, either due to weather, terrain, or other reasons, it was not always suited to the scenario.[150] As a result, most of the early Marine Hueys were equipped as armed variants to fill the assault support role. The small turning radius and payload characteristics made the UH-1E a convenient gun platform. Hueys equipped with TK-2 rocket- and machine-gun kits were ideal for a variety of uses, from escorts to close-air support and command and control.[151] Huey gunships did not change Marine helicopter doctrine, but they added another valuable member to the air-ground team and increased the overall effectiveness of helicopter operations.[152]

Jonathan F. Abel Collection, Archives Branch, Marine Corps History Division

Commandant Leonard F. Chapman (center) receives a briefing at Marble Mountain on the armed UH-1E.

By mid-April, the White House believed the situation in Vietnam had deteriorated to the point that "something new must be added in the South to achieve victory."[153] The administration was reluctant to deploy more forces, as it was aware of the lack of popular and congressional support. Following a civilian-military leadership conference in Honolulu, the conferees agreed that another 48,000 personnel should deploy to the Republic of Vietnam.[154] In early May, the Joint Chiefs of Staff received the president's approval to send additional Marine ground and aviation units to Da Nang. On 6 May 1965, III Marine Expeditionary Force (redesignated Marine Amphibious Force, or III MAF, the following day) superseded 9th MEB.[155] III MAF could now absorb the full 3d Marine Division as well as the 1st MAW. Having provided administrative and logistical support to Marine helicopter operations in Vietnam from its headquarters in Okinawa since 1962, the aircraft wing moved to Da Nang on 11 May 1965. Brigadier General Keith B. McCutcheon, a decorated aviator and key figure in the development of the Marine helicopter program, arrived two weeks later to assume command of the 1st MAW.[156]

General Westmoreland advised the commanding general of III MAF, Major General William R. Collins, that his mission was multifaceted: coordinate the defense of three bases with the ARVN; support the South Vietnamese military; maintain the ability to conduct patrols, offensive operations, and reserve reaction missions; and carry out contingency plans as directed by USMACV. Expanding the rotary-wing aviation mission, the Marine Corps introduced the Special Landing Force. A self-sustaining strategic contingency force, it offered a water-

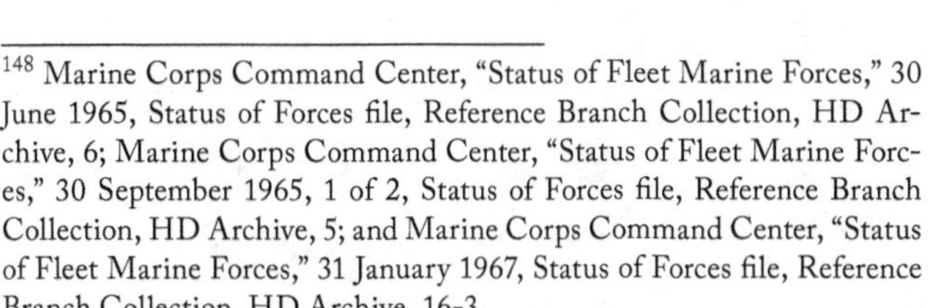

148 Marine Corps Command Center, "Status of Fleet Marine Forces," 30 June 1965, Status of Forces file, Reference Branch Collection, HD Archive, 6; Marine Corps Command Center, "Status of Fleet Marine Forces," 30 September 1965, 1 of 2, Status of Forces file, Reference Branch Collection, HD Archive, 5; and Marine Corps Command Center, "Status of Fleet Marine Forces," 31 January 1967, Status of Forces file, Reference Branch Collection, HD Archive, 16-3.

149 Fails, *Marines and Helicopters, 1962–1973*, 109–11.

150 LtCol D. K. Tooker, USMC, "Now We're Shooting Back," *Marine Corps Gazette* 50, no. 5 (May 1966): 46.

151 Maj Gary L. Telfer, USMC; LtCol Lane Rogers, USMC; and V. Keith Fleming Jr., *U.S. Marines in Vietnam: Fighting the North Vietnamese, 1967* (Washington, DC: History and Museums Division, Headquarters, U.S. Marine Corps, 1984), 206.

152 Tooker, "Now We're Shooting Back," 46.

153 As quoted in Drea, *McNamara, Clifford, and the Burdens of Vietnam*, 30.

154 Drea, *McNamara, Clifford, and the Burdens of Vietnam*, 29–31.

155 Shulimson and Johnson, *The Landing and the Buildup, 1965*, 35–36; and *USMC/Vietnam Helicopter Association: Pop a Smoke*, 13.

156 Shulimson and Johnson, *The Landing and the Buildup, 1965*, 35–36.

Boeing-Vertol CH-46 Sea Knight

The Boeing-Vertol CH-46 Sea Knight's roots trace to the YHC-1B, a turbine-powered assault helicopter designed by Vertol for a U.S. Army competition in 1956. To address Marine Corps requirements, the company made substantial changes to the aircraft's structure and components, leading to the HRB-1.

Defense Department (Marine Corps) A422475

The Marines began testing the aircraft in April 1962. The production version—designated CH-46A and referred to by Marines as the "forty-six" and then the "Phrog" following the Vietnam War—made its first flight at Vertol's plant in mid-October 1962. Capable of carrying a 4,000-pound payload of combat troops (between 17 and 20 when combat loaded) or cargo, the aircraft had a range of 100 nautical miles and a cruising speed of 130 knots. With its emergency water landing and takeoff capability, rear loading ramp, and folding rotors, the Sea Knight was capable of both field and amphibious operations.

The first CH-46A arrived in the fleet in 1964. Demand for more helicopters in Southeast Asia brought the first examples to Vietnam on 8 March 1966 when 24 from HMM-164 landed at Marble Mountain Air Facility (Da Nang East Air Field), a welcome arrival for UH-34 crews flying war-weary aircraft. The Sea Knight immediately increased the lift capability of helicopter squadrons and earned praise for its payload capacity and ease of loading and unloading.

HMM-265, the second squadron to fly CH-46s, arrived at Marble Mountain in May. By the close of 1966, two more squadrons began operating from Ky Ha, bringing the total to nearly 80 Sea Knights in the Republic of Vietnam; at the height of the war, there were more than 100. Catastrophic structural failures in the aft pylons of some aircraft led to tragic accidents in 1967, forcing the emergency grounding of all CH-46s. Boeing-Vertol responded with a modification program conducted in Japan that required 1,000 hours of work per airframe. By the start of 1968, most of the improved aircraft were back with their squadrons. The changes eventually led to the introduction of the CH-46D, a dependable and long-serving aircraft.[1]

[1] "Vertol Helicopter Chosen for Marines," *Aviation Week* 74, no. 9 (27 February 1961): 33; "Marine CH-46A Designed for Ship, Field Operations," *Aviation Week* 77, no. 19 (5 November 1962): 108; William H. Gregory, "Vertol Flys [*sic*] CH-46A Assault Helicopter," *Aviation Week* 77, no. 17 (22 October 1962): 30; "Marines' New Helo Flies," *Naval Aviation News*, December 1962, 2; and Jack Shulimson, *U.S. Marines in Vietnam: An Expanding War, 1966* (Washington, DC: History and Museums Division, Headquarters, U.S. Marine Corps, 1982), 263–64.

borne and heliborne strike capability as part of the U.S. Seventh Fleet's amphibious arm. As a strategic reserve, the SLF consisted of an infantry battalion landing team, naval surface assault craft, and a medium helicopter squadron. Vertical lift from ships provided the SLF greater flexibility and maneuverability than its land-based counterparts. Beginning operations in June 1965 from USS *Iwo Jima* (LPH 2), Colonel Ewers's HMM-163 was the first in a regular rotation of medium helicopter squadrons flying from on board ship.[157]

Marine Helicopters in 1965

Marine Commandant General Wallace M. Greene Jr. characterized 1965 as "a year of action for the Marine Corps."[158] It was also a year of growth and expansion. The rapid buildup of U.S. personnel, including Marine fixed-wing squadrons, crowded the airfield at Da Nang in spring 1965. For Marine Aviation in general, lack of adequate space was the principal factor limiting the deployment of more units to Vietnam.[159] To address the need, the Marines constructed a new airfield east of Da Nang on a stretch of beach along the Han River. The cantonment and airfield were situated between a large green peak called Monkey Mountain to the north and the brown-gray Marble Mountain to the south.[160] Elements of the 9th Marines secured the area in the early summer while members of a naval construction battalion (Seabees) built the aircraft group's helicopter installation on the beach.[161]

From their new base, the Marines had an unobstructed view of the South China Sea. The ocean breeze held the mosquitos at bay, which were a persistent annoyance for those in Da Nang. Despite the idyllic scene, oppressive heat and blowing sand remained inescapable. Sandbagged bunkers, concertina wire, and minefields were a reminder that the Viet Cong were active in the area and that helicopters on the ground were inviting targets. A runway running north-south separated two helicopter revetment areas and tactical air crew quarters for MAG-16.[162]

When the 9th MEB came ashore at Da Nang in March 1965, the Department of the Navy authorized the Marine Corps 433 helicopters. The Service's force structure included 398 rotorcraft spread across 20 squadrons, 14 of which were medium transport squadrons.[163] Throughout June and July, helicopter squadrons made a series of moves that tilted the Marine Corps' balance of rotary-wing aviation toward Asia, illustrating the growing demands of the air-ground team in the Republic of Vietnam. HMM-161 arrived from Marine Corps Air Station Kane'ohe Bay, Hawai'i, in June. Nine days later, HMM-261 deployed to Da Nang from Marine Corps Air Station New River. By 26 August, construction of the new Marble Mountain Air Facility, or Da Nang East Airfield, progressed enough that MAG-16 and its Da Nang-based squadrons completed the five-kilometer move to their new beachside home from the overcrowded air base. HMM-161 divided its UH-34s into two detachments: 14 aircraft at Phu Bai and 10 at Qui Nhon. Between the four medium helicopter squadrons and the one observation squadron, the Marine helicopter fleet operating in the country totaled 107 helicopters: 95 UH-34D Seahorses and 12 UH-1E Hueys.[164]

Maxwell Taylor, who served as U.S. ambassador to the Republic of Vietnam from 1 July 1964 to 14 July 1965 after retiring from the U.S. Army, and his successor, Henry Cabot Lodge Jr., joined Secretary McNamara on a visit to the Republic of Vietnam on 16 July 1965. After consulting Westmoreland, the group concluded that South Vietnamese military forces were not capable of reducing Viet Cong attacks without further assistance. President Johnson announced another manpower increase on 28 July, nearly doubling the number of U.S. personnel in Vietnam to 125,000. For the Marine Corps, this set into motion the reinforcement of III

157 In the first three years of operations, medium helicopter squadrons in the combat theater rotated between the Special Landing Force (SLF) and the aircraft groups stationed in the Republic of Vietnam. Organizational changes in late 1968, however, made HMM-163, HMM-362, and eventually HMM-265 permanently tasked with SLF duty. The SLF's amphibious assault ship was also made up of a rotation of USS *Iwo Jima* (LPH 2), USS *Valley Forge* (LPH 8), USS *Princeton* (LPH 5), USS *Okinawa* (LPH 3), and USS *Tripoli* (LPH 10).

158 Gen Wallace M. Greene Jr., USMC, "Commandant's Report," *Marine Corps Gazette* 50, no. 5 (May 1966): 21.

159 McCutcheon, "Marine Aviation in Vietnam," 128.

160 Bob Stoffey, *Cleared Hot!: A Marine Combat Pilot's Vietnam Diary* (New York: St. Martin's Press, 1992), 9.

161 Shulimson and Johnson, *The Landing and the Buildup, 1965*, 65.

162 Shulimson and Johnson, *The Landing and the Buildup, 1965*, 149; Stoffey, *Cleared Hot!*, 53–54; and Fails, *Marines and Helicopters, 1962–1973*, 93.

163 Fails, *Marines and Helicopters, 1962–1973*, 2, 92.

164 Fails, *Marines and Helicopters, 1962–1973*, 92, 186; and Report, Marine Corps Command Center, "Status of Fleet Marine Forces," 30 August 1965, Status of Forces file, Reference Branch Collection, HD Archive, 5, 24.

DA NANG REGION, 1965–71

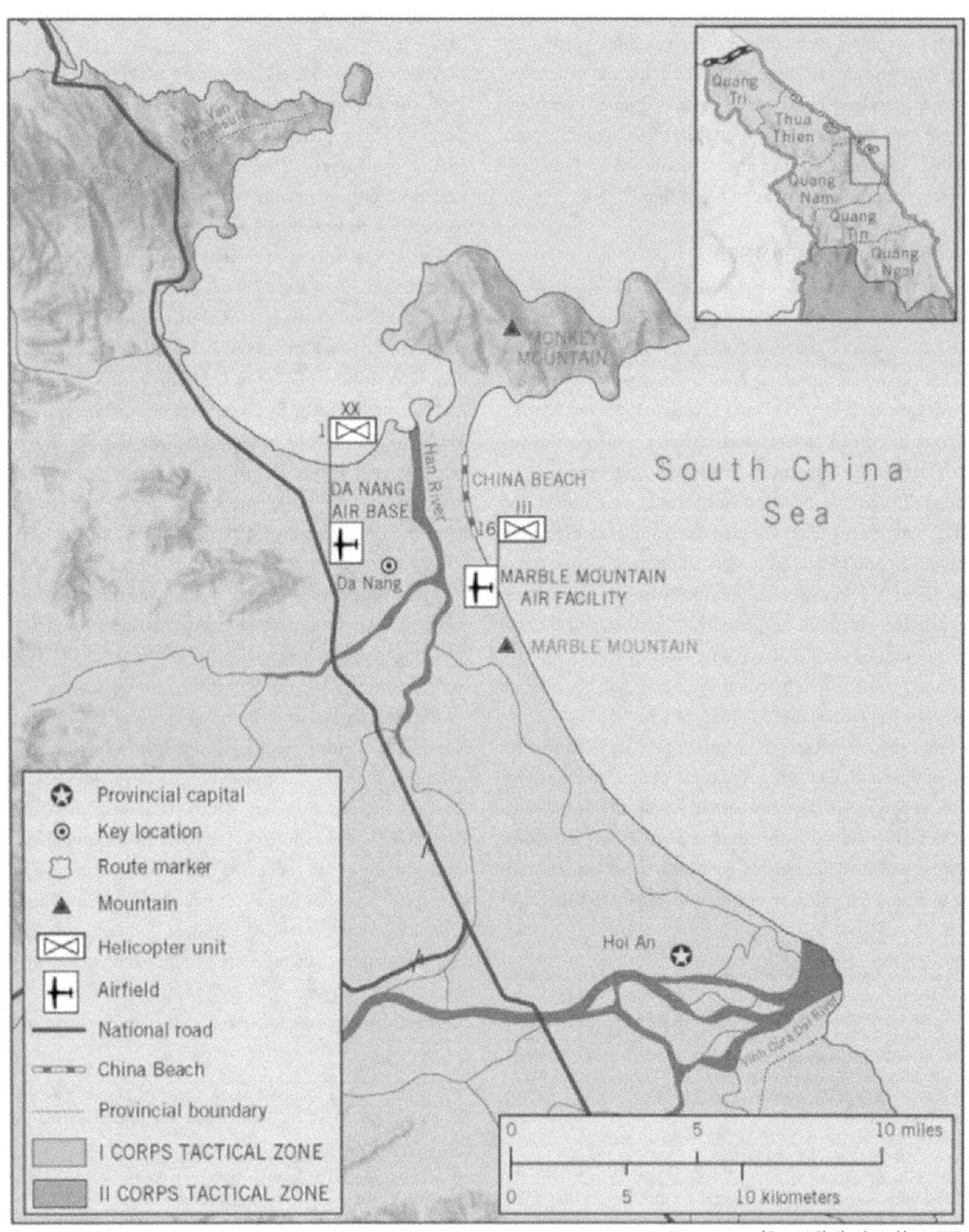

Map courtesy of Pete McPhail, adapted by MCUP

Roy E. Moss Collection, Archives Branch, Marine Corps History Division

Marble Mountain Air Facility.

Defense Department (Marine Corps) A374440

UH-34s from HMM-261 refuel at Da Nang after returning from an operation, July 1965.

MAF with the 7th Marines' regimental headquarters and two battalions. Major General Lewis W. Walt, having succeeded Major General Collins as commander of III MAF in June, received permission in July to conduct search and clear operations against the Viet Cong. The arrival of the 7th Marines would enable the Marines to exploit helicopter mobility and employ the air-ground team in Vietnam in their first major Marine offensive against the Viet Cong.[165]

Operation Starlite

In mid-1965, intelligence sources revealed that the Viet Cong was gathering in strength throughout southern I Corps.[166] Evidence showed that elements of the *1st Viet Cong Regiment*, a main force unit, and a company of local guerrillas was moving toward the U.S./ARVN enclave at Chu Lai. More information suggested that this enemy concentration was near the coast, 19 kilometers from the air base at Chu Lai, and potentially preparing to attack U.S. and ARVN forces there. MAG-16 helicopters—including HMM-162, HMM-163, HMM-365 operating from within the RVN, and HMM-161 on USS *Princeton* beginning in May 1965—flew multiple sorties in support of ground forces around the base, hauling external loads of materiel to construct defensive positions in anticipation of enemy attacks.[167]

The Viet Cong had built a stronghold at the center of the Van Tuong Peninsula that provided fighting positions, supply depots, and hideaways.[168] The 3d Battalion, 3d Marines, began conducting small patrols in the area in July. Regular enemy contact necessitated increasing the patrols to company-size. As of mid-August, the quality of the enemy contacts indicated the arrival of main force Viet Cong on the peninsula, the first professional and well-trained units the Marines encountered.[169]

On 30 July, Westmoreland made it clear that he expected the Marines to launch operations to find and engage the enemy alongside ARVN troops. With ample evidence to suggest an imminent the *1st Viet Cong Regiment* attack on Chu Lai, Major General Walt decided on 15 August to launch a preemptive attack on the Van Tuong Peninsula. III MAF settled on a combined amphibious and heliborne search and destroy operation with ARVN in the area, codenamed Operation Star-

[165] Shulimson and Johnson, *The Landing and the Buildup, 1965*, 65.

[166] Central Intelligence Agency Monthly Report, "The Situation in South Vietnam," 4 June 1965, box 2, folder 1, Larry Berman Collection, item no. 0240201018, TTU Vietnam Archive, 4; and Central Intelligence Agency Monthly Report, "The Situation in South Vietnam," 4 August 1965, box 7, folder 113, Central Intelligence Agency Collection, item no. 04107113002, TTU Vietnam Archive, 4.

[167] Stoffey, *Cleared Hot!*, 27.

[168] Andrew, *The First Fight*, 7–8.

[169] Andrew, *The First Fight*, 8–9.

lite.[170] In light of the threat now facing Chu Lai, and with the opportunity to face a large contingent of enemy forces, Westmoreland gave Major General Walt permission to rewrite the engagement instructions to support offensive operations.[171]

Operation Starlite was a combined heliborne and amphibious assault with air, artillery, and naval fire support. Plans called for a company from 3d Battalion, 3d Marines, to land in the early morning north of the Van Tuong village complex. They would act as a blocking force for elements disembarking from LVTP-5 amphibious armored fighting vehicles (amtracs) onto the beach to the south and drive northeast. The rest of the 3d Battalion was slated to make an amphibious landing later in the day, establishing a beachhead before pushing inland to take high ground and turn northward with a platoon of tanks following the infantry assault. Arriving by helicopters, 2d Battalion, 4th Marines, would assault to the west of the initial engagement area and sweep northeast to link up with 3d Battalion, 3d Marines.[172]

For the first time in the Republic of Vietnam, Marine rotary-wing aircraft used vertical envelopment doctrine in a sizeable operation as part of a Marine air-ground team. HMM-261 and HMM-361 from Marble Mountain provided helicopter support with 26 UH-34s.[173] Gunship escorts for the transports came from VMO-2 as well as eight U.S. Army UH-1Bs, while Marine Aircraft Group 11 (MAG-11) and MAG-12 provided close-air support in the assault area. The medium helicopter squadrons would assault into multiple landing zones to the west of Highway 1 on 18 August, delivering infantry from 2d Battalion, 4th Marines, to the fight.[174] Meanwhile, two artillery batteries from 3d Battalion, 12th Marines, from Chu Lai provided fire support. One headed south by ground while the other moved by helicopter. The U.S. Navy destroyers USS *Orleck* (DD 886) and USS *Pritchett* (DD 561) as well as the cruiser USS *Galveston* (CLG 3) were waiting to provide additional long-range fires.[175]

Warren Smith Collection, Archives Branch, Marine Corps History Division

Army UH-1B gunships escort UH-34Ds from HMM-364 in 1964.

At 1700 on 17 August, Marines from Company M, 3d Battalion, 3d Marines, disembarked from amtracs onto the beach, beginning Operation Starlite. The Marines reached their blocking positions before dawn on 18 August and dug in.[176] Well into the night, the remainder of the battalion loaded aboard ships in preparation for their landing while strafing runs from Douglas A-4 Skyhawks prepared the beach.[177] In the predawn darkness at Chu Lai airstrip, HMM-261 and HMM-361 of MAG-16 waited for the 2d Battalion to load aboard Seahorses while air support from MAG-11 and MAG-12 and artillery prepared the landing zones. Taking off at 0630, Company G, 2d Battalion, 4th Marines, rode on board the first wave of helicopters on the 15-minute flight to their objective and landed unopposed at LZ Red. Company E arrived at LZ White in a second wave at 0730 and took fire from a ridgeline one kilometer to the northeast. Making the short trip from Chu Lai, Company H assaulted from LZ Blue in a third wave at 0745.[178]

170 III Marine Amphibious Force (III MAF) After Action Report for Operation Starlite, 31 August 1965, pt. 1, box 48, folder 14, MACV Historical Office Documentary Collection, item no. F015800480104, TTU Vietnam Archive, 2–3.
171 Shulimson and Johnson, *The Landing and the Buildup, 1965*, 69.
172 Andrew, *The First Fight*, 11, 15.
173 III MAF After Action Report for Operation Starlite, 2; and Stoffey, *Cleared Hot!*, 55.
174 Stoffey, *Cleared Hot!*, 55.
175 Andrew, *The First Fight*, 13.
176 Shulimson and Johnson, *The Landing and the Buildup, 1965*, 72.
177 Andrew, *The First Fight*, 17–18.
178 Andrew, *The First Fight*, 25–26.

OPERATION STARLITE INITIAL ASSAULTS, 18 AUGUST 1965

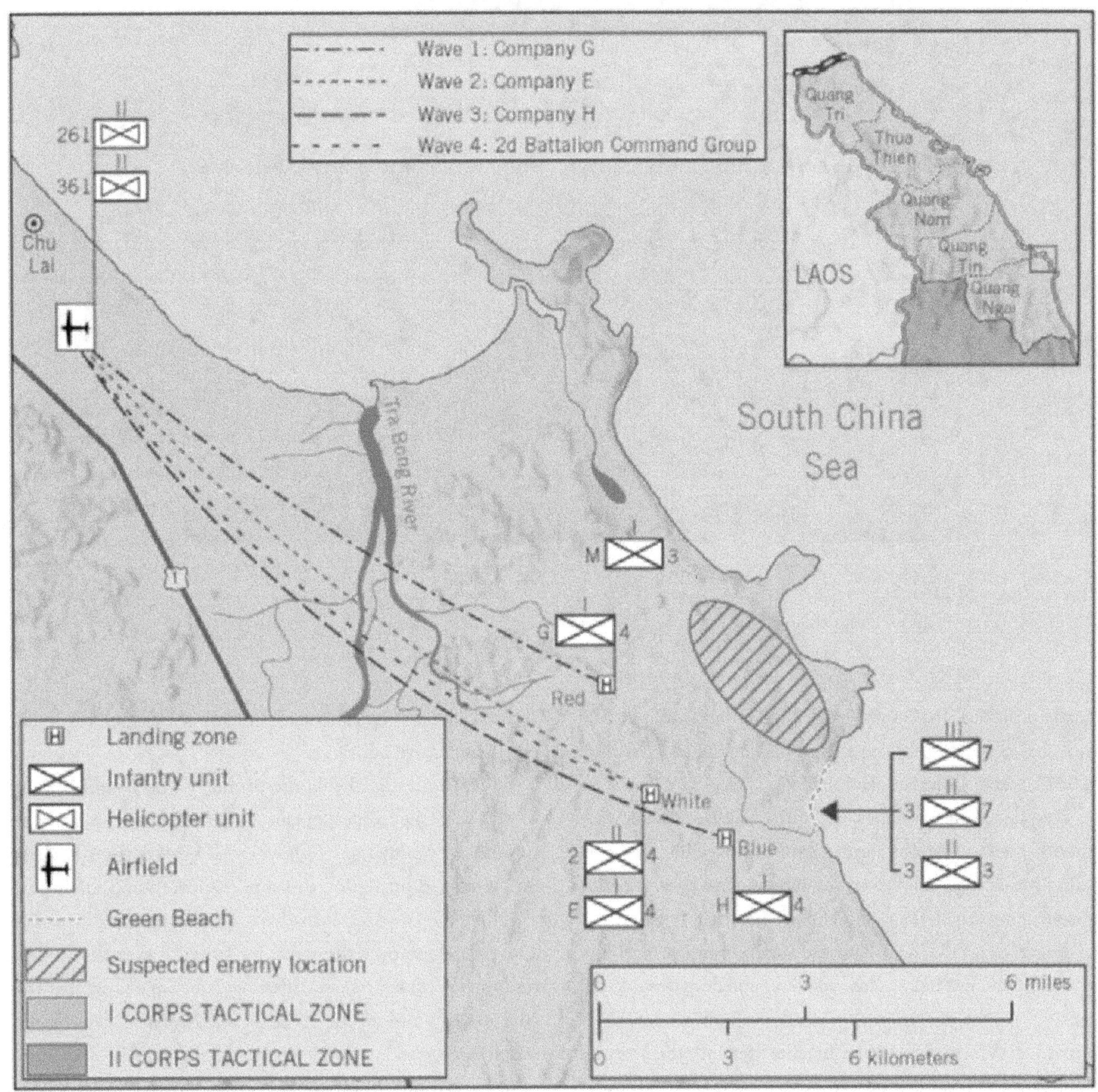

Map courtesy of Pete McPhail, adapted by MCUP

Rice paddies, woods, streams, and hedgerows dotted the otherwise flat terrain. A small knoll referred to by the Marines as Hill 43 rose near the landing zone farthest to the south, only a few hundred meters east of LZ Blue, south of the village of Nam Yen. Company H inadvertently dropped nearly inside the perimeter of the *60th Viet Cong Battalion*, who were positioned on Hill 43. With enemy fire pouring down on LZ Blue from the nearby hillock, fixed-wing attack aircraft attempted to neutralize Viet Cong positions. Gunships from VMO-2 and Army UH-1Bs from Quang Ni also flew runs against the

Defense Department (Marine Corps) A801303

Chu Lai, December 1965.

enemy positions. The fourth wave of the initial assault arrived with the 2d Battalion command group, landing at LZ White at 0815, where Company E waited.[179]

Despite taking casualties, the initial Marine assaults went smoothly, as the first lifts surprised the enemy while they were eating breakfast.[180] However, the subsequent waves encountered enemy small-arms and mortar fire that targeted the landing zones. HMM-361 pilot Captain Howard B. Henry reported, "You just had to close your eyes and drop down to the deck."[181] As the operation developed, the heaviest resistance was at LZ White, as 50–60 insurgents fired into the Marines from elevated positions on the ridgeline. At 0830, Companies E and G attacked northeast from the landing zones and secured villages that contained unmanned but well-concealed enemy defensive positions.[182]

With the initial heliborne assault phase complete, two of the three helicopter squadrons left the area to conduct normal daily activities.[183] Only 18 UH-34Ds from HMM-361 remained on station to support Operation Starlite. Just as its MAG-16 sister units departed, the fighting increased and calls came over the radio for casualty evacuations and resupply. With resistance stiffening, it became clear that the Marines had located the *1st Viet Cong Regiment*. During the initial casevac and resupply missions, helicopters took the first of numerous hits. One Seahorse crashed on the beach. More than an hour after the last wave of the initial assault landed, the situation necessitated HMM-163 bring in Company I

[179] Otto J. Lehrack, *The First Battle: Operation Starlite and the Beginning of the Blood Debt in Vietnam* (Havertown, PA: Casemate Publishers, 2004), 81; Andrew, *The First Fight*, 13; and 1st MAW ComdC, July and August 1965, pt. 3, folder 67, U.S. Marine Corps History Division Vietnam War Documents Collection, item no. 1201067188, TTU Vietnam Archive, 13.

[180] Andrew, *The First Fight*, 26.

[181] As quoted in Shulimson and Johnson, *The Landing and the Buildup, 1965*, 75.

[182] Andrew, *The First Fight*, 23.

[183] SSgt Cory D. Overstreet, interview with SSgt Herbert W. Chennault (undated), Interview #529 (HMM-361), Marine Corps Oral History Collection, HD Archive, hereafter Overstreet interview.

Sikorsky UH-34D "YN-19"

With its retirement from the Marine Corps active inventory, UH-34D Bureau Number (BuNo) 150570 arrived in an Arizona boneyard in 1972. For decades, the airframe baked in the desert sun, a shell stripped of its major components. In 2001, however, Alan Weiss, a retired Vietnam-era CH-53 Sea Stallion crew chief and head of the Marine Helicopter Squadron 361 Veterans Association, rescued BuNo 150570 from the scrap heap. Former Seahorse crews, other operators, and businesses donated time, parts, and services to support a lengthy restoration in a New York barn. In 2005, BuNo 150570 returned to the air for a second career as a flying memorial, making appearances at dozens of public and private events.

Rising operating costs, however, led the association to donate it to the National Museum of the Marine Corps. In November 2013, it made a final flight to Quantico, Virginia, to become a permanent exhibit. Now the centerpiece of a static display in the Leatherneck Gallery, BuNo 150570 depicts a singular moment in Marine Corps history, an assault by members of Company H, 2d Battalion, 4th Marines, landing at LZ Blue on 18 August 1965 during Operation Starlite.

The helicopter wears the tail code and aircraft number YN-19, the same identifier it had in 1965 as an HMM-361 helicopter during Starlite. BuNo 150570's logbooks trace its service in Vietnam from July 1964 to May 1969. Numerous pilots and crews logged hours in the aircraft while assigned to 11 different squadrons, including three separate tours with HMM-363. In its final retirement, BuNo 150570 stands as a tribute to every Marine helicopter squadron that served in Vietnam, memorializing the service, commitment, and sacrifice made by all Marines.[1]

Courtesy of the author

[1] Ben Kristy, "Sikorsky UH-34D," National Museum of the Marine Corps, accessed 31 May 2020.

from 3d Battalion, 7th Marines, part of the SLF on board USS *Iwo Jima*.[184]

The Viet Cong fighters organized their defense and used small arms, automatic weapons, mortars, and recoilless rifles. Fourteen of HMM-361's 18 aircraft took hits by the afternoon.[185] Approximately 10 of those suffered extensive damage, yet the pilots managed to bring the aircraft back home. Maintenance crews at Marble Mountain cannibalized the

[184] Andrew, *The First Fight*, 35, 37.

[185] MAG-16 ComdC, 15 September 1965, encl. 6, folder 77, U.S. Marine Corps History Division Vietnam War Documents, item no. 1201077204, TTU Vietnam Archive, 2.

more damaged helicopters to keep others flying. Aircraft continued to respond to calls for casevacs throughout the afternoon. According to Staff Sergeant Cory Overstreet, crew chief on HMM-361's commanding officer's UH-34D, "As quick as they got one into flying condition, they would launch again. Maybe with a different crew, whoever was available at the time."[186] In total, three MAG-16 squadrons and HMM-163 flew more than 500 sorties on the first day of Operation Starlite.[187]

The battle raged for the next few days, offering many pilots "action-packed flight time," as HMM-361 pilot Captain Bob Stoffey termed it.[188] Of the many heroic actions of helicopter pilots during the operation, Major Donald J. Reilly from VMO-2 displayed uncommon valor and devotion to his fellow Marines. During his initial sortie on the first day of the operation, Major Reilly's armed UH-1E Huey was "hit by intense ground fire," requiring him to make an emergency landing in the battle area. Company I from the SLF provided security while Major Reilly made quick repairs. Lifting off again, he returned the aircraft and crew safely to base. Without hesitation, he climbed aboard another Huey and immediately flew back to the fight.[189]

Reilly acted as a forward air controller for jets, directing them in the relief of an amphibian tractor supply column pinned down. Ground fire again damaged his aircraft, wounding the gunner. Returning to Marble Mountain, he took the controls of a third Huey and flew south. With no casevac helicopters nearby, Reilly answered an emergency evacuation call for three wounded Marines and landed in heavy enemy fire. After taking considerable damage, he was uncertain how much longer the helicopter would fly. Unable to communicate directly with the ground forces, he decided to return to Marble Mountain. Reilly attempted to rejoin the battle for a fourth time, but no aircraft were available—VMO-2 was already at maximum effort, and he had damaged one-third of the squadron's UH-1Es.[190]

For his "calm courage under fire and inspiring devotion to duty" during Operation Starlite, Reilly received the Distinguished Flying Cross.[191] On multiple occasions in the months after the battle he showed continued courage, receiving the Bronze Star, the Silver Star, and the Air Medal with Gold Stars for numerous missions from April to November. On 9 December 1965, Reilly was killed in Quang Tin Province during Operation Harvest Moon. His actions that night led to a posthumous Navy Cross.[192] "He was not fearless," claimed his commanding officer, "but he always had the courage to do what he thought must be done in spite of the risks involved." An "excellent pilot" who proved his heroism repeatedly during 298 missions and 133 casualty evacuations, the 38-year-old officer's "actions against the enemy were highly effective, but he derived his satisfaction from saving lives of our wounded troops by flying them out of the frontlines, and not from the devastations he was forced to wreak on the enemy."[193]

Operation Starlite produced other heroic moments by Marine aviators. First Lieutenant Richard J. Hooten from HMM-361 was not supposed to fly at the start of the oper-

Jack Dyer Collection, Archives Branch, Marine Corps History Division

In flight with a UH-1E gunship.

[186] Overstreet interview, audio beginning at 22:30.
[187] 1st MAW ComdC, July and August 1965, pt. 3, 13.
[188] Stoffey, *Cleared Hot!*, 55.
[189] Andrew, *The First Fight*, 39.
[190] MAG-16 ComdC, 15 September 1965, 3.
[191] "Donald Joseph Reilly," Valor.MilitaryTimes, Distinguished Flying Cross Citation, accessed 3 March 2022.
[192] MAG-16 ComdC, 15 September 1965, encl. 6, 2.
[193] United States Marine Corps News Release, No. JMG-170-66, 25 August 1966, box 16, folder 2, Gen Keith B. McCutcheon Papers, HD Archive, 1–3.

ation, as he was the squadron maintenance test officer for the day. Learning of the deteriorating situation, however, he climbed aboard a UH-34D and flew toward LZ White, arriving around 0745. One Marine helicopter flew into a maelstrom in response to a casevac request. Breaking off his final approach, the pilot called over the radio, "Rolling out. Too hot, too hot, I can't land." Hooten reacted quickly, responding, "This is Tarbush [HMM-361] aircraft. Rolling in, rolling in."[194] Once in the LZ, Hooten and his crew braved enemy fire while infantry loaded wounded Marines, the first casevac of Operation Starlite. Two more times, he and his crew barely returned to safety. On the first occasion, his Seahorse took multiple hits. With wounded on board, Hooten struggled with the helicopter as it lost hydraulic power en route to *Iwo Jima*. He returned to the battle area later in the day in another helicopter, only to sustain substantial damage again, forcing him to turn back to Chu Lai with wounded crewmembers on board. Hooten continued flying supply and casevac missions in a third aircraft, actions for which he received a Distinguished Flying Cross.[195]

As the largest operation in the war to date that relied on vertical envelopment doctrine, Operation Starlite was a test for the air-ground team. For the most part, the consensus within the Marine Corps was that the helicopters proved rugged and dependable. They played a critical role providing supplies and troops as needed. MAG-16 suffered seven casualties on the first day, the majority of them pilots.[196] More than 75 percent of the aircraft in HMM-361 that started the first day took hits requiring field repairs but were able to get back into the fight. The Marines proved that when called on, rotary-wing aircraft were not as fragile as detractors might claim.[197]

Operation Starlite also illustrated the flexibility of the helicopter units. While only HMM-361, HMM-261, and VMO-2 were slated to participate in the assault, MAG-16 ultimately employed all five of its squadrons. They flew missions around the clock until the ground combat elements returned to Chu Lai via helilift. The units from Da Nang and Hue/Phu Bai, as well as the SLF squadron, illustrated what was possible when ground- and sea-based rotary-wing elements from the air-ground team coordinated. Flying off USS *Iwo Jima*, HMM-163 took over resupply and casualty evacuation responsibilities from HMM-361. During a week on the Van Tuong Peninsula, its 23 UH-34s flew nearly 3,000 sorties, conducted almost 200 casualty evacuations, ferried reinforcements, and provided thousands of tons of supplies for fellow Marines.[198]

Operation Starlite also showed what vertical envelopment could achieve against significant Communist forces. Helicopters quickly placed infantry on the ground at key points, a tactical necessity given the insurgents' swift mobility. The initial Marine assault caught the enemy somewhat unprepared, resulting in an uncoordinated and ineffective response during the critical early hours of the battle on 18 August. Had the landings taken longer, the *1st Viet Cong Regiment* could have mounted a stronger defense at the landing zones. Given more time, they might have chosen to either evacuate the peninsula or send for reinforcements. However, the tactical advantage the helicopters provided denied the enemy the ability to commit to either option until it was too late, enabling the Marines to badly maul one of the enemy's best regiments.[199]

The victory came at a cost, however. Fifty-four Americans lost their lives during the operation and around 200 were wounded. The Marines counted 614 enemy killed, providing American planners with data that they could use as a quantifiable measure of success.[200] Body counts aside, Operation Starlite disrupted a planned Viet Cong attack on the new helicopter installation at Chu Lai. Moreover, the operation displayed the effectiveness of firepower and mobility as part of Westmoreland's conventional warfare approach and proved that U.S. forces could pin down and engage the elusive Viet Cong in set-piece battles.

Marine Aircraft Group 36 Arrives

A year after the planned June 1964 withdrawal of Marine helicopters from the Republic of Vietnam, the Marine Corps deployed the largest number of rotary-wing units in Service history to that point. While MAG-16 supported ground com-

---

194 Overstreet interview, audio beginning ca. 08:30.

195 Lehrack, *First Battle*, 110.

196 MAG-16 ComdC, 15 September 1965, encl. 6, 12.

197 Lehrack, *First Battle*, 111.

198 Andrew, *The First Fight*, 40.

199 MAG-16 ComdC, 15 September 1965, encl. 6, 2; and Andrew, *The First Fight*, 52, 53.

200 Shulimson and Johnson, *Landing and Buildup*, 80; and Lehrack, *The First Battle*, 181.

Defense Department (Marine Corps) A422065

Infantry of the 2d Battalion, 4th Marines, board UH-34Ds of HMM-363 on USS *Iwo Jima*. Medium helicopter squadrons rotated between ground bases and the Special Landing Force during their deployments to Southeast Asia.

bat elements in Operation Starlite, a second aircraft group steamed across the Pacific Ocean en route to Vietnam. MAG-36, under the command of Colonel William G. Johnson, deployed from Marine Corps Air Facility Santa Ana on 11 August 1965 on board USS *Princeton*.[201]

MAG-36 was comprised of HMM-362, HMM-363, HMM-364, VMO-6, and a detachment of heavy-lift Sikorsky CH-37Cs from Headquarters and Maintenance Squadron 16. The group arrived at Da Nang on 3 September, along with HMM-163 on board USS *Iwo Jima* as part of the Special Landing Force. The 1st MAW now had two aircraft groups operating helicopters in Vietnam. Between them were seven medium helicopter squadrons, two observation squadrons, and the partial headquarters and maintenance squadron, more than 200 helicopters in total.[202] The Marine Corps had 19,000 personnel in the Republic of Vietnam in June 1965; by September of that year, there were more than 35,000 Marines in-country.[203]

The increases in personnel required additional facilities within I Corps. In July, the Marines opened a base at Qui Nhon, 280 kilometers south of Da Nang. The enclave at Qui Nhon supported Marine helicopter operations far from the expansive aviation bases to the south. A detachment of 10 aircraft from HMM-161 traveled more than 300 kilometers from

[201] Marine Aircraft Group 36 (MAG-36) ComdC, 13 October 1965, folder 78, U.S. Marine Corps History Division Vietnam War Documents, item no. 1201078261, TTU Vietnam War Archive.

[202] Report, Marine Corps Command Center, "Status of Fleet Marine Forces," 30 September 1965, Status of Forces file, Reference Branch Collection, HD Archive; and *USMC/Vietnam Helicopter Association: Pop a Smoke*, 79.

[203] Report, Marine Corps Command Center, "Status of Fleet Marine Forces," 30 June 1965, Status of Forces file, Reference Branch Collection, HD Archive; and "Status of Fleet Marine Forces," 30 September 1965.

TABLE 1. 1ST MAW HELICOPTER UNITS AND HELICOPTERS IN SOUTHEAST ASIA, DECEMBER 1965

MAG-16 Marble Mountain Air Facility		MAG-36 Ky Ha Air Facility		SLF USS *VALLEY FORGE*	
Unit	Aircraft number/type	Unit	Aircraft number/type	Unit	Aircraft number/type
VMO-2	20—UH-1E	VMO-6	18—UH-1E	HMM-261	23—UH-34D
HMM-361	17—UH-34D	HMM-362	24—UH-34D		
HMM-263	17—UH-34D	HMM-364	24—UH-34D		
HMM-161 (Phu Bai Airfield)	24—UH-34D	HMM-363 (Qui Nhon Airfield)	24—UH-34D		
Sub Unit 1, H&MS-16	5—CH-37				

Source: Report, Marine Corps Command Center, "Status of Fleet Marine Forces," 31 December 1965, pt. 1, Status of Forces file, Reference Branch Collection, Archives Branch, Marine Corps History Division, Quantico, VA.

Phu Bai to Qui Nhon to support the reinforced 2d Battalion, 7th Marines.[204] In early September Marines broke ground on a new helicopter base in preparation for MAG-36's arrival. The Ky Ha Air Facility was 80 kilometers south of Da Nang on the Ky Ha Peninsula in Quang Tin province.[205] Unlike Chu Lai's shimmering sand, Ky Ha was made up of red laterite soil that became sticky mud when wet. MAG-36's arrival coincided with the start of monsoon rains that unleashed a torrent that turned the base into a veritable bog. While less than ideal, the facility meant that by the end of 1965, Marine helicopters could operate from four base areas in addition to the SLF: Marble Mountain, Hue-Phu Bai, Ky Ha, and Qui Nhon.

Marine Helicopters in 1966

As the new year approached, Major General Walt recommended to General Westmoreland and USMACV an increase in Marine infantry battalions from 12 to 18. Walt wanted to pursue what he called a balanced strategy in I Corps that included defending bases, conducting offensive operations against the Viet Cong, and dismantling Communist infrastructure in villages through civic programs and local security (also termed *pacification*).[206] Walt's strategy was to establish security enclaves and then expand them until the areas under Marine and ARVN control were linked.[207] Before Walt could implement the approach, however, North Vietnamese infiltration into the demilitarized zone during the first half of 1966 forced III MAF to move the 3d Marine Division into the hills and mountains of Quang Tri Province to serve as a blocking force.[208]

The Marines called the effort to push back NVA incursions the "DMZ war." The first large 3d Marine Division effort

[204] Andrew, *The First Fight*, 4; *USMC/Vietnam Helicopter Association: Pop a Smoke*, 13; and LtCol Gary W. Parker, USMC, *A History of Marine Medium Helicopter Squadron 161* (Washington, DC: History and Museums Division, Headquarters, U.S. Marine Corps, 1978), 23.

[205] The Republic of Vietnam government created Quang Tin Province out of a portion of Quang Nam Province in July 1962. The Communist government dissolved the province and returned the area to Quang Nam after the end of the war. Fails, *Marines and Helicopters, 1962–1973*, 93, 186.

[206] BGen Edwin H. Simmons, "Marine Corps Operations in Vietnam, 1965–1966," in *The Marines in Vietnam, 1954–1973: An Anthology and Annotated Bibliography*, 2d ed. (Washington, DC: History and Museums Division, Headquarters, U.S. Marine Corps, 1985), 56.

[207] This spreading of security out from multiple centers was the so-called inkblot approach. See David Strachan-Morris, *Spreading Ink Blots from Da Nang to the DMZ: The Origins and Implementation of U.S. Marine Corps Counterinsurgency Strategy in Vietnam, March 1965 to November 1968* (Warwick, UK: Helion and Company, 2020).

[208] Jack Shulimson, *U.S. Marines in Vietnam: An Expanding War, 1966* (Washington, DC: History and Museums Division, Headquarters, U.S. Marine Corps, 1982), 314.

was Operation Hastings. Starting on 15 July and lasting until 3 August, it attempted to stop enemy troops from funneling south through the Ngan Valley. A Marine task force composed of four infantry battalions, an artillery battalion, and supporting elements attacked North Vietnamese regulars 40 kilometers west of Dong Ha near a 200-meter-tall feature, known as the Rockpile, that towered above Route 9. At 0745, CH-46A Sea Knights from HMM-164 and HMM-165 inserted 3d Battalion, 4th Marines, at Landing Zone Crow, eight kilometers northeast of the Rockpile. The landing zone proved too small for the 20 helicopters and two Sea Knights, which collided and crashed while a third struck a tree. Two Marines were killed and seven injured in the accidents. Later in the day, enemy antiaircraft fire shot down a CH-46, killing 13 and wounding 3.[209]

During the next two weeks, HMM-161, HMM-163, HMM-164, and HMM-265 transported infantry troops throughout the area of operations in pursuit of NVA fighters, who withdrew at the end of July. While Operation Hastings was a tactical victory for the Americans, III MAF recognized that it would have to keep units in the rugged areas of northern I Corps. By summer and fall 1966, 1st Marine Division conducted pacification operations in the coastal lowlands while 3d Marine Division waged large-unit operations in the hills and mountains of northern I Corps, requiring helicopter squadrons to support both.[210]

Commandant Greene reported to the Senate in 1966 how crucial he believed helicopters were to Marine operations in Vietnam. "The validity of the vertical assault concept," he argued, "has been combat-proven without a doubt." The capabilities of helicopters made them the Marine Corps' single-largest aviation investment in Vietnam, causing the ratio of fixed-wing to rotary-wing aircraft to be "higher than would normally be the case if we were engaged in assault amphibious operations." Along with the successes of fixed-wing units, the air-ground team "has once again been reaffirmed and our combat experienced level in both departments is rising rapidly." Although the Marine Corps developed helicopter assault techniques for amphibious assaults, Greene asserted "it is obvious that they make us capable of other types of warfare, and give us great flexibility of employment."[211]

Combat Sorties for HMM Squadrons

Given that helicopter combat operations were a relatively new element of warfare, the Marine squadrons in Vietnam continually developed new tactics and techniques. The procession of units and operational areas brought fresh insights. Successive squadrons rotating to Vietnam typically reviewed previous units' reports before deploying, informing the way that they operated once arriving in the combat zone and helping them acclimate.

Pilots and their crews flew an average of four to eight hours a day performing various missions. The majority were logistical runs that included resupplying Marine or ARVN outposts scattered across I Corps, transporting personnel, or evacuating the sick and wounded. Although routine, they were no less tiring for personnel who usually flew multiple sorties a day, loaded and unloaded their aircraft repeatedly, and made refueling stops. Pilots learned that even routine resupply missions sometimes required aggressive flying outside of prescribed peacetime maneuvers. Crews typically considered the area around landing zones to be relatively secure because of the perimeter established by the ground units they were resupplying. This cone of safety extended from between 600 and 900 meters above the landing zone and a 300-meter radius around it. Even if on a single-ship resupply mission, pilots found it best to just "get on down there," according to HMM-362 pilot First Lieutenant D. Larry Fraser.[212]

The preferred method of flying into these situations was to descend directly from above, minimizing exposure time outside the cone. Starting at a high altitude, one or two pilots at a time initiated a steep descent into the landing zone. Cutting the throttle, lowering the nose of the aircraft, and starting a tight 360-degree turn, pilots yawed, or rotated, their

[209] Shulimson, *An Expanding War, 1966*, 159–65.

[210] Jack Shulimson and Maj Edward F. Wells, "First In, First Out: The Marine Experience in Vietnam, 1965–71," in *The Marines in Vietnam, 1954–1973*, 27. See also Edward Thomas Nevgloski, "Understanding the United States Marines' Strategy and Approach to the Conventional War in South Vietnam's Northern Provinces, March 1965–December 1967" (PhD diss., King's College London, 2019), 266–74.

[211] Greene, "Commandant's Report," 25–27.

[212] Larry Fraser, interview with Stephen Maxner, 5 February 2001, Oral History Interview transcript, Larry Fraser Collection, item no. OH0027, TTU Vietnam Archive, 15, hereafter Fraser interview.

Jack Dyer Collection, Archives Branch, Marine Corps History Division

Marine patrols often depended on logistical support from helicopters, such as this HMM-263 aircraft delivering rations in 1966.

helicopters into the turn.[213] Moving sideways through the air presented the broad fuselage to the wind, reducing the aerodynamic efficiency and resulting in a rapid descent. As the ground approached, pilots rolled in throttle and rebalanced the aircraft before touching down. This method worked well in small, isolated zones. Major Vincent J. Guinee, maintenance officer for HMM-261 and HMM-361 in 1965–66, recalled, "We had very few problems with that type of approach."[214]

Combat assaults, or strikes, provided an antidote to the tedium of resupply flights. In terms of enemy resistance, strikes were "the worst," according to Sergeant William J. Jackson of HMM-161. In I Corps in early 1966, the enemy was usually waiting. "If you don't catch fire on the first drop into the zone," Jackson advised, "you can almost bet they'll be shooting at you the second or third time around."[215] Soon after returning from Vietnam in 1966, HMM-163's commanding officer, Lieutenant Colonel Norman Ewers, saw strikes as the most exciting and rewarding missions his squadron flew, the type that everyone looked forward to. On those operations, the Marines "came to grips with the enemy."[216] Deeper into their deployments, they gathered more insights about their area of operations and the enemy, turning pilots into savvy combat aviators. "You learned that if you flew on this side of this particular mountain you'd likely get shot at," remembered First Lieutenant Fraser. Marine aviators naturally "learned a little more" every time they went out, "and you were better at the end of your tour than you were at the beginning."[217]

Pilots approached landings during strikes differently than resupply missions, as they were often setting down into unfamiliar areas in enemy-held territory. They found that the best method was to land in flights of four if there was sufficient room. As in the Shufly era, fixed-wing aircraft and helicopter gunships would soften the landing zone with preparatory fires. Once any enemy were suitably suppressed, the transport helicopters made their final approach. The performance capabilities of Huey gunships influenced Marine tactics. Although the UH-1s were powerful for their size, they were limited in airspeed, forcing the UH-34Ds to fly slower than 100 knots on final approach so that the escorts could keep up. Spiraling into landing zones was not feasible because the gunships could not aim their forward-fixed guns at the ground in steep turns. Instead, the Seahorses flew straight into the landing zone, allowing the UH-1Es flying alongside to fire their guns and rockets to suppress the zone. For reconnaissance Marines, thick jungle sometimes prevented conventional landings. Pilots were forced to hover their aircraft over narrow openings in the trees when extracting small patrol teams from triple-canopy forest. Crews deployed a ladder that the troops could climb up to enter the aircraft, or to which they could attach themselves for extraction.[218]

[213] Don Chretien, *Hovering in Harm's Way: A Marine Corps Pilot's Journey to Vietnam and Back* (n.p.: CreateSpace, 2017), 24.

[214] Maj Vincent J. Guinee, interview with SSgt Herbert W. Chennault (undated), Interview #530 (HMM-261, HMM-361), Marine Corps Oral History Collection, HD Archive, audio beginning ca. 05:30, hereafter Guinee interview.

[215] Frank Beardsley, "HMM-161," *Leatherneck* 50, no. 2 (February 1966): 34–35.

[216] Col N. G. Ewers, interview with Maj E. J. Godfrey, 30 March 1966, Interview #94A (HMM-163), Marine Corps Oral History Collection, HD Archive.

[217] Fraser interview, 15.

[218] Charles R. Smith, *U.S. Marines in Vietnam: High Mobility and Standdown, 1969* (Washington, DC: History and Museums Division, Headquarters, U.S. Marine Corps, 1988), 256–57. See also Bill Peters, *First Force Recon Company: Sunrise at Midnight* (New York: Presidio Press, 1999); and Michael Lee Lanning and Ray W. Stubbe, *Inside Force Recon: Recon Marines in Vietnam* (Guilford, CT: Stackpole Books, 2017).

Jack Dyer Collection, Archives Branch, Marine Corps History Division

A UH-34 lands on a casualty evacuation mission in 1966. Marine Corps helicopters flew 2,000 such sorties in 1965, climbing to 35,000 the following year.

Jack Dyer Collection, Archives Branch, Marine Corps History Division

A UH-34 delivers a wounded Marine to medical teams on board the hospital ship *Repose* in 1966.

Emergency casualty evacuation missions were also common for helicopter crews, and oftentimes the most personally rewarding and important. Depending on their location and condition, pilots would take wounded troops to a medical facility either in the Republic of Vietnam or to a hospital ship anchored off the coast. The movement of patients from battlefields to medical facilities by aircraft significantly improved the chances of survival. Although the U.S. military first proved the concept in the Korean War and the U.S. Army fielded air ambulance helicopter units in the Republic of Vietnam, it was not something for which most Marine pilots received formal training in the 1960s. The principal field manual that guided Marine rotary-wing units, *Helicopterborne Operations*, FMFM 3-3, contained less than one page on casualty evacuations.[219] Crews learned most procedures through experience and conversations with other pilots, while sometimes the knowledge passed somewhat more formally from squadron to squadron.[220] Marine Corps aircraft flew more than 194,000 casualty evacuation missions from 1966 through 1971 that saved countless lives.[221]

Helicopter Pilot Shortage

The successes of medium helicopter squadrons in Vietnam brought increased demand for pilots. Unfortunately, four years of rotating helicopter pilots and crews through the Republic of Vietnam stretched the pool of aviation personnel to its limits by 1966. A little more than half of the 4,200 Marine pilots were members of fixed-wing tactical squadrons while the rest were spread throughout staff positions that required aviation expertise. Casualties also took a toll on the available number of

[219] *Helicopterborne Operations*, FMFM 3-3 (Washington, DC: Headquarters United States Marine Corps, 1966).

[220] LtCol Frank E. Allgood, "MED-EVAC: Vietnam Style," *Marine Corps Gazette* 52, no. 8 (August 1968): 36.

[221] Helmet E. Dost, *Marine Corps and Army Helicopter Employment and Attrition Statistics for Southeast Asia Operations from October 1965 through December 1971*, vol. 2, Study 1008 (Arlington, VA: Center for Naval Analyses, October 1972), 5.

Defense Department (Navy) 1142213

HMM-362 helicopters on board USS *Iwo Jima* in the South China Sea, February 1967.

personnel filling helicopter billets. Between the start of Shufly and April 1967, 719 pilots and crew members were injured or killed in the Republic of Vietnam.[222]

Between mid-1965 and mid-1966, the Marine Corps increased its requirements from 4,307 pilots to 5,292. Plans for additional helicopter squadrons would require as many as 800 new aviators undergoing flight training in Pensacola, Florida, annually.[223] At the start of 1967, a total of 11 helicopter squadrons operated in Vietnam between the 2 aircraft groups and the SLF, each presenting a complicated shuffle of personnel between tours.[224] As Brigadier General McCutcheon admitted to Major General Walt at III MAF in late 1966, the "biggest single problem in aviation continues to be pilots. There just isn't any instant way to get more."[225]

222 Fails, *Marines and Helicopters, 1962–1973*, 137.

223 Fails, *Marines and Helicopters, 1962–1973*, 131.

224 Telfer, Rogers, and Flemming, *Fighting the North Vietnamese, 1967*, 206.

225 Letter from MajGen Keith B. McCutcheon to LtGen Lewis W. Walt, 29 October 1966, box 16, folder 2, Gen Keith B. McCutcheon Papers, HD Archive, 1.

With such a large percentage of the Marine helicopter personnel pool serving in Southeast Asia and the unrelenting demand for crews, many pilots faced the likelihood of multiple deployments to the Republic of Vietnam before their fixed-wing colleagues deployed to the theater for the first time.[226] The combat workload also put considerable pressure on crews. The helicopter units of the 1st MAW in I Corps supported Marine, U.S. Army, and ARVN troops, giving pilots little rest between missions.[227] Compared to a Marine jet aviator's 250 sorties per 13-month tour, helicopter pilots could expect more than 1,100. During large operations, helicopter pilots averaged 15.5 hours crew time per day for up to 10 days.[228]

The Commandant was aware of the unyielding demand for officers with specific qualifications, such as helicopter pilots, and he knew that meant "inconveniences, personal hardship,

226 Shulimson, *An Expanding War, 1966*, 262.

227 Jack Shulimson et al., *U.S. Marines in Vietnam: The Defining Year, 1968* (Washington, DC: History and Museums Division, Headquarters, U.S. Marine Corps, 1997), 570.

228 Fails, *Marines and Helicopters, 1962–1973*, 133, 137.

Keith B. McCutcheon

General Keith B. McCutcheon laid the foundation for the Marine rotary-wing force that flew in Vietnam, earning him the sobriquet, "Father of Helicopters." Born in East Liverpool, Ohio, in 1915, he graduated in 1937 with a degree in management engineering from Carnegie Institute of Technology in Pennsylvania and accepted an appointment as a second lieutenant in the Marine Corps that same year. After graduating from flight school in July 1940, he spent a year with Marine Observation Squadron 1. McCutcheon attended postgraduate aeronautical engineering school at the U.S. Naval Academy in Annapolis, Maryland, and graduated at the top of his class in 1943. He then continued his education at the Massachusetts Institute of Technology and earned a master's degree.

Promoted to lieutenant colonel in September 1944, McCutcheon became operations officer in Marine Aircraft Group 24 in the Southwest Pacific. While there, he developed procedures for air-ground coordination between the U.S. Army and Marine Corps, a significant contribution to the war in the Pacific that earned McCutcheon the Legion of Merit. A courageous pilot in combat, he was awarded a Silver Star, a Distinguished Flying Cross, and six Air Medals before returning to the United States in November 1945.

Receiving orders to command Marine Helicopter Squadron 1 at Quantico in July 1950, within weeks he had taken helicopter training and qualified faster than any naval aviator to that point. He took over ongoing experiments with helicopters and was vocal about their potential in amphibious warfare. He soon took command of the pioneering Marine Helicopter Transport Squadron 161, which was establishing tactics and techniques through combat experience in Korea.

After earning another Legion of Merit and four more Air Medals, McCutcheon spent three years at Quantico as chief of Air Section, Marine Corps Equipment Board. After attending the National War College in 1960 in Washington, DC, McCutcheon served first as assistant, and then as director of aviation. He returned to the Pacific in 1963, eventually joining the staff of the commander in chief, Pacific Command, where he again worked on Joint air operation procedures as the war in Vietnam escalated, earning him a third Legion of Merit.

As one of the most knowledgeable and experienced Marine Aviation officers, in June 1965 McCutcheon took command of the 1st Marine Aircraft Wing and also became deputy commander, III Marine Amphibious Force. After a promotion to major general, he returned to Washington as deputy chief of staff (air) in mid-1966. The stresses of his final assignments, and a battle with terminal cancer, sapped him of his normally inexhaustible energy. Appointed Assistant Commandant of the Marine Corps in 1970, his poor health kept him from assuming the position. Promoted to the rank of general in July 1971, McCutcheon passed away less than two weeks later.[1]

[1] LtCol William R. Fails, USMC, *Marines and Helicopters, 1962–1973* (Washington, DC: History and Museums Division, Headquarters, U.S. Marine Corps, 1978), 105–8.

and sacrifices."[229] These harsh realities made continued service unappealing for some, especially when compared to promising commercial aviation careers. In 1966, Marine aviators saw their obligated service rise from three to three-and-a-half years. Two years later, the Marine Corps increased it again to four-and-a-half years. Yet another fixed-wing pilot transition

[229] As quoted in Fails, *Marines and Helicopters, 1962–1973*, 139.

program further unsettled Marine aviation.[230] In 1967, nearly 290 Reserve pilots left the Marine Corps and 107 requested retirement. The Marines lost an additional 125 aviators who either died or were captured while serving in Vietnam. Finally, 257 pilots voluntarily resigned their commissions. The combined losses totaled 777 Marine pilots by year's end. While 573 students graduated flight school that year, the Marine Corps was still short 706 aviators by June 1967. Even after reducing the number of pilots required to 5,002, the Marine Corps faced a shortage of 851 pilots by February 1968, some 416 of those helicopter aviators.[231]

Lieutenant General Krulak characterized the problem as a "disease," at least in part related to a dip in morale across the ranks. Writing to McCutcheon, who by then was a major general and deputy chief of staff (air), Krulak related that pilot "retention is an all-hands effort, having to begin with a bone-deep conviction that we need these young officers as an essential fraction of the Marine Corps."[232]

Major General McCutcheon's attempts to increase the number of aviator billets met with a tepid response from within the Navy and the Office of the Secretary of Defense. Revealing his frustration with the issue, he wryly wrote to the 1st MAW commanding general that if they "had a pilot for each piece of paper we have written on this there would be no shortage."[233] The Marine Corps opted to implement creative stopgap measures to address the issue. Funneling all available pilots to operational units was a quick fix that stood the chance of buying time to recruit and train new cohorts. However, planners believed eliminating or substituting billets would provide the largest number of pilots. They carefully scoured aviation-related positions throughout the ranks to determine which could be dissolved. In the end, McCutcheon and his staff identified 709 billets that they believed should be transferred to helicopter squadrons. The Marines also identified aviation-related billets that ground officers could fill to free up pilots, including generals' aides and squadron staff positions, which created another 245 openings.[234]

In an effort to ease the pressure on helicopter units, the Marine Corps abandoned plans to expand its wartime strength. Keeping the helicopter squadrons in the Western Pacific at peacetime pilot strength would avoid adding requirements for 166 additional personnel. Offering only 20 days of leave for pilots who were deploying to or returning from Vietnam produced the equivalent of 102 more aviators. Finally, the Marine Corps skeletonized its Atlantic fleet commitments and transferred personnel to Vietnam.[235]

The Marine Corps' management efforts averted disaster but ultimately failed to solve the problem. The only answer was to find a way to produce more pilots inside existing structures. A solution appeared in summer 1967 when spaces opened in the U.S. Air Force's fixed-wing classes slated for West German students. The Marine Corps filled the gap by shifting some of its fixed-wing training load from Naval Air Station Pensacola to U.S. Air Force training bases, freeing up spots at Pensacola for helicopter pilot instruction. Using that template, McCutcheon and Secretary McNamara's offices worked out an arrangement with the U.S. Army to provide rotary-wing instruction to Marine pilots as part of its regular instruction rotation.[236]

The Marine Corps candidates received primary training at Fort Wolters, Texas, from civilian instructors alongside Army aviators. The next phase of their training occurred at either the Army's main aviation facilities at Fort Rucker, Alabama, or Hunter Army Airfield in Georgia. The first Marines completed the joint program in September 1968. Nearly 150 others followed by the end of fiscal year 1969. The extra training capacity was a crucial turning point for the Marine Corps helicopter program, providing noticeable relief to the pilot shortage.[237]

Crew Chiefs and Gunners

While officers served as pilots, Marine helicopter operations also depended on the expertise and dedication of enlisted crew. Crew chiefs kept aircraft in good mechanical order so that

[230] Fails, *Marines and Helicopters, 1962–1973*, 140.

[231] Fails, *Marines and Helicopters, 1962–1973*, 132–33. The combined losses add up to 779, but the source states 777.

[232] Letter from LtGen Victor H. Krulak to MajGen Keith B. McCutcheon, 19 June 1967, box 18, folder 2, Gen Keith B. McCutcheon Papers, HD Archive, 2.

[233] Letter from MajGen Keith B. McCutcheon to MajGen L. B. Robertshaw, 2 February 1967, box 18, folder 2, Gen Keith B. McCutcheon Papers, HD Archive, 1.

[234] Fails, *Marines and Helicopters, 1962–1973*, 139.

[235] Fails, *Marines and Helicopters, 1962–1973*, 139.

[236] Fails, *Marines and Helicopters, 1962–1973*, 141–42.

[237] Fails, *Marines and Helicopters, 1962–1973*, 142–43.

Stephen W. Pless

Medal of Honor Citation

Stephen W. Pless Collection, Archives Branch, Marine Corps History Division

Left to right, GySgt Leroy N. Poulson, LCpl John G. Phelps, Capt Rupert E. Fairfield, and then-Capt Stephen W. Pless.

Major Stephen W. Pless was born 6 September 1939 in Newnan, Georgia. He graduated from the Georgia Military Academy in 1957, when he joined the Marine Corps Reserve. Finishing flight training in 1960, Pless served with Marine Light Helicopter Transport Squadron 262 (HMR[L]-262) and HMR(L)-264 during the next two years before receiving orders to join the second Shufly squadron, HMM-162. Returning to the United States as a basic flight instructor at Pensacola, he earned a promotion to captain in 1964. Redeploying to Vietnam in 1966, he received a Bronze Star and the Korean Order of Military Merit after assignments with Republic of Korea units. Pless received a Silver Star and Distinguished Flying Cross for his actions while serving as assistant operations officer of Marine Observation Squadron 6 (VMO-6) from March to September 1967. He is the only Marine aviator awarded the Medal of Honor in the Vietnam War, which he received for his courageous conduct while rescuing American soldiers.[1] Pless died in a motorcycle accident in Pensacola in July 1969.

PLESS MEDAL OF HONOR CITATION

The President of the United States of America, in the name of Congress, takes pleasure in presenting the Medal of Honor to Major Stephen Wesley Pless (MCSN: 0-79156), United States Marine Corps, for conspicuous gallantry and intrepidity at

[1] "Medal of Honor Award Case File—Stephen Wesley Pless," Tim Frank Collection, item no. 18700254001, TTU Vietnam Archive.

the risk of his life above and beyond the call of duty on 19 August 1967, while serving as a helicopter gunship pilot attached to Marine Observation Squadron SIX (VMO-6), Marine Aircraft Group THIRTY-SIX, First Marine Aircraft Wing, in action against enemy forces near Quang Nai, Republic of Vietnam. During an escort mission Major Pless monitored an emergency call that four American soldiers stranded on a nearby beach were being overwhelmed by a large NLF [National Liberation Front] force. Major Pless flew to the scene and found 30 to 50 enemy soldiers in the open. Some of the enemy were bayoneting and beating the downed Americans. Major Pless displayed exceptional airmanship as he launched a devastating attack against the enemy force, killing or wounding many of the enemy and driving the remainder back into a tree line. His rocket and machinegun attacks were made at such low levels that the aircraft flew through debris created by explosions from its rockets. Seeing one of the wounded soldiers gesture for assistance, he maneuvered his helicopter into a position between the wounded men and the enemy, providing a shield, which permitted his crew to retrieve the wounded. During the rescue the enemy directed intense fire at the helicopter and rushed the aircraft again and again, closing to within a few feet before being beaten back. When the wounded men were aboard, Major Pless maneuvered the helicopter out to sea. Before it became safely airborne, the overloaded aircraft settled four times into the water. Displaying superb airmanship, he finally got the helicopter aloft. Major Pless' extraordinary heroism coupled with his outstanding flying skill prevented the annihilation of the tiny force. His courageous actions reflect great credit upon himself and uphold the highest traditions of the Marine Corps and the United States Naval Service.

they could stand up to the extreme punishment of combat. These noncommissioned officers were 19- or 20-years old on average. Despite their youth, they were experts on all components of complicated rotary-wing machinery, and their expertise and professionalism were vital to the success of Marine helicopters in Vietnam. Most received training as mechanics and then attended advanced schooling in the United States to become crew chiefs, accruing thousands of hours of experience. Their duties included diagnosing in-flight malfunctions, acting as loadmaster for cargo and passengers, operating the aircraft hoist, communicating with the pilots at all times to improve spatial awareness outside the helicopter, refueling the aircraft between missions, and serving as door gunners.[238]

Crew chiefs spent up to 16–20 hours each day around their assigned aircraft, more than any other member of the crew, including pilots.[239] They flew missions during the day and spent many nights completing preventive maintenance and system checks in preparation for the following day. If the helicopter took damage during a mission, crew chiefs made repairs before the next flight. As a result, they got little sleep during large operations that lasted for days or weeks.

Helicopter crews established close relationships during their service. "It was quite an exciting life," according to HMM-163 pilot First Lieutenant Carl E. Bergman. "You lived right on the edge of dying all the time." Flying 12–14 hours a day, either assaulting into hostile landing zones or operating in dangerous weather and terrain, built tight bonds and lasting relationships between crew members.[240] Pilots became close to their crew chiefs, holding immense respect for their professionalism, work ethic, dedication, and capabilities. Major Guinee was "forever amazed while I was over there at the performance of our mech[anic]s and crew chiefs." To Guinee, it "just amazed me how they stood up under the conditions."[241] According to UH-34D pilot Captain Bill Collier, "the machines would have deteriorated to un-flyable junk

[238] Ronald E. Winter, *Masters of the Art: A Fighting Marine's Memoir of Vietnam* (New York: Presidio Press, 2005), 92.
[239] 1stLt Coleman D. Kuhn Jr., Marine Corps History Division Oral History, Interview #3683 (VMO-6), Marine Corps Oral History Collection, HD Archive, beginning ca. 11:00, hereafter Kuhn interview.
[240] Carl E. Bergman, interview with Sean Passaro, 30 January 2005, Carl E. Bergman Collection (AFC/2001/001/28630), Veterans History Project, American Folklife Center, Library of Congress, Washington, DC, video starting ca. 18:00.
[241] Guinee interview, audio starting ca. 14:00.

Jonathan F. Abel Collection, Archives Branch, Marine Corps History Division

UH-1Es and an OV-10 Bronco of VMO-2 in a MAG-16 hangar at Marble Mountain, 1968. Maintenance personnel and crew chiefs routinely worked through the night to prepare aircraft for missions the following day.

in less than a week" without the efforts of their crew chiefs.[242] Almost universally, Marine helicopter pilots reported mid-tour that their crew chiefs deserved more recognition for their efforts.[243] "These were the most dedicated crews that could possibly have existed, anywhere, anytime, any war," reflected Collier.[244]

Gunners generally held the rank of private first class or lance corporal. The job was secondary to their main duties, which were usually noncombat roles. Spurred on by the allure of extra flight pay, most were also attracted by the excitement that came with flight operations.[245] There was also some exclusivity to the position, as only a set number from each job assignment could fly as door gunners each month. Corporal Ronald E. Winter, an avionics expert, was eager to get airborne soon after arriving in Vietnam in 1968. "I really wanted to be part of the battle," he recalled. "I wanted to fly. I wanted to fly all the time, and I wanted to be where the action was."[246]

Riding in the cabin behind the pilots, helicopter crew chiefs and gunners had little protection. Each was issued a flak jacket. The prevailing belief was that the nylon and fiberglass plates were most effective at stopping shrapnel and bullets penetrating the underside of the aircraft, so many crew sat on the jackets rather than wearing them. While most crewmembers felt safe inside their aircraft, the same feeling did not apply to ground troops. "As brave as they were," according to Winter, "a lot of grunts hated being in the helicopters when

[242] Capt Bill Collier, USMCR, *The Adventures of a Helicopter Pilot: Flying the H-34 Helicopter in Vietnam for the United States Marine Corps* (Sandpoint, ID: Wandering Star Press, 2014), viii.

[243] Kuhn interview, audio starting ca. 11:40.

[244] Collier, *The Adventures of a Helicopter Pilot*, viii.

[245] Chretien, *Hovering in Harm's Way*, 40.

[246] Winter, *Masters of the Art*, 136.

Jonathan F. Abel Collection, Archives Branch, Marine Corps History Division

Pfc Sam Hampton examines an enemy round lodged in his helmet after flying as a gunner on an HMM-161 CH-46.

Jonathan F. Abel Collection, Archives Branch, Marine Corps History Division

CH-46s from HMM-262 fly above I Corps as crew chief Cpl Arnold E. Duseberg looks out the starboard side.

we started taking hits, because they generally couldn't fire back and there was nowhere to go for cover."[247] Crewmen, however, had plenty of opportunities to return fire. Despite the number of aircraft remaining steady, combat sorties for 1st MAW CH-46s rose 80 percent between 1966 and 1967. That figure jumped another 250 percent by 1968 as the war involved more conventional operations against big units, and especially during the multiphase Tet Offensive.[248]

Marine Helicopters in 1967–68

North Vietnamese regular units continued to infiltrate the DMZ in late 1966 to undermine III MAF's pacification efforts by drawing Marines away from the population centers and toward the border areas.[249] These attacks compelled the Pentagon to devise an unmanned anti-infiltration area in September 1966.[250] The plan called for a deforested barrier stretching along the DMZ from the Laotian border to the South China Sea. American forces sowed minefields and monitored enemy ground activity with air patrols as well as seismic and motion detectors.[251] In the east, 1st Marine Division constructed firebases along the eastern border areas of I Corps while 3d Marine Division built defenses in the west along

247 Winter, *Masters of the Art*, 134.

248 Dost, *Marine Corps and Army Helicopter Employment and Attrition Statistics for Southeast Asia Operations from October 1965 through December 1971*, vol. 2, 35–38.

249 Vo Nguyen Giap, "The Big Victory, the Great Task," *Quan Doi Nhan Dan*, 14–16 September 1967.

250 *McNamara, Clifford, and the Burdens of Vietnam*, 126–30.

251 As the plan originated with Secretary McNamara and his Office of the Secretary of Defense, it quickly earned the nickname the "McNamara Line" or "McNamara Wall." See Michael Rühle, "The Rise and Fall of the 'McNamara Line': Enduring Lessons from the Vietnam War," *Comparative Strategy* 37, no. 5 (2018): 404–13.

Route 9.[252] The North Vietnamese directed their attention toward the firebases and spent the first half of 1967 attempting to turn the enclaves into "isolated islands in the open sea of people's war."[253]

General Walt disagreed with the barrier concept from the start, arguing that III MAF lacked the necessary manpower to support the system. Marine commanders posited that a mobile defense was more flexible and economical.[254] Barrier construction progressed despite the Marine's objections, and the 3d Marine Division was to conduct clearing operations and construct the eastern sector of the barrier by November 1967.[255] Due to a lack of resources and guidance, USMACV ultimately failed to fully implement the anti-infiltration concept. In August 1967, General Westmoreland ordered the Marines to stop work on the barrier system in the east, and 1st Marine Division turned its attention to repelling NVA infiltrations. The 3d Marine Division in the west built a strongpoint defense of mutually supporting firebases. By the end of 1967, the entire division was deployed near the DMZ, with the bulk of its combat power in the western reaches of Quang Tri Province. They protected Route 9 and blocked a suspected infiltration route that the NVA could use to outflank III MAF and invade RVN provinces to the south.[256]

Defense Department (Marine Corps) 3D-5-3270-68

CH-46s carry elements of 4th Marines into the demilitarized zone near the Ben Hai River, September 1968.

Khe Sanh

In early 1967, the NVA continued a significant buildup of forces in the northwestern part of the country. Enemy activity increased in a hilly area 25 kilometers south of the demilitarized zone near the village of Khe Sanh. Situated in a picturesque valley, the isolated hamlet would have been mostly disconnected from the war, except that it sat along Route 9. A network of trails and roads fed the main highway, which ran from the mountains of Laos to the coastal plains of Quang Tri Province.[257] Three kilometers north of the village, 6,000 Marines and ARVN Rangers occupied a combat base from which they conducted border surveillance and curbed enemy infiltration into the Republic of Vietnam. The installation was on level ground and enjoyed good fields of fire, despite sitting in a U-shaped bowl ringed by lushly vegetated hills that peaked between 600–900 meters above Route 9.[258]

Khe Sanh Combat Base supported various outposts that dotted the surrounding hills, serving as the focal point of the interdiction mission. These garrisons were the eyes and ears of the Marines monitoring enemy movement into the

[252] Shulimson et al., *The Defining Year, 1968*, 86–94.

[253] DIA Intelligence Supplement, "General Vo Nguyen Giap's Present View of the War," 25 September 1967, box 13, folder 18, Glenn Helm Collection, TTU Vietnam Archive. For the battles, see Col Joseph C. Long, USMCR (Ret), *Hill of Angels: U.S. Marines and the Battle for Con Thien, 1967 to 1968*, Marines in the Vietnam War Commemorative Series (Quantico, VA: Marine Corps History Division, 2016); and Col Rod Andrew Jr., USMCR, *Hill Fights: The First Battle of Khe Sanh, 1967*, Marines in the Vietnam War Commemorative Series (Quantico, VA: Marine Corps History Division, 2017).

[254] Telfer, Rogers, and Flemming, *Fighting the North Vietnamese, 1967*, 88.

[255] Shulimson and Wells, "First In, First Out," 28.

[256] Shulimson and Wells, "First In, First Out," 27–28; and Simmons, "Marine Corps Operations in Vietnam, 1968," in *The Marines in Vietnam, 1954–1973*, 102.

[257] Marion F. Sturkey, *Bonnie-Sue: A Marine Corps Helicopter Squadron in Vietnam* (Plum Branch, SC: Heritage Press International, 1999), 412.

[258] Shulimson et al., *The Defining Year, 1968*, 59–60; and Capt Moyers S. Shore II, USMC, *The Battle for Khe Sanh* (Washington, DC: History and Museums Division, Headquarters, U.S. Marine Corps, 1969), 8–10.

KHE SANH REGION, 1968

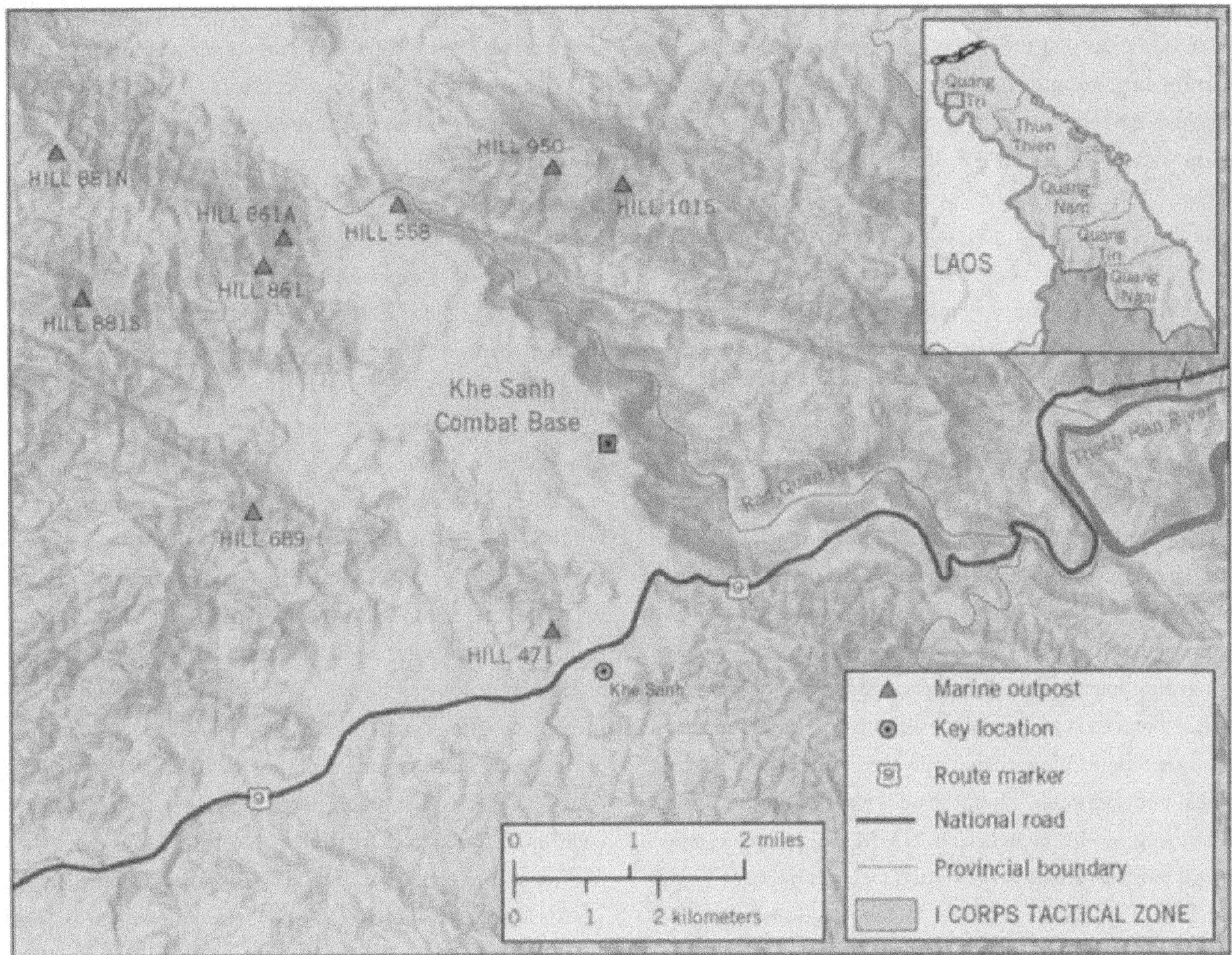

Map courtesy of Pete McPhail, adapted by MCUP

Republic of Vietnam. Perched high above the combat base, Marines could look down onto the nearby valleys, roads, and trails that facilitated cross-border movement.[259] Khe Sanh's airstrip, which the French built years earlier, sat atop a high plateau, two sides of which dropped hundreds of meters down to a river below. With the nearest Marine base, Dong Ha, a 50-kilometer drive on Route 9 across rugged terrain, the 1,200-meter runway was the installation's lifeline for supplies and replacements.[260]

Fighting in spring 1967 in the mountains around Khe Sanh combat base was bloody for the Marine units, costing 155 killed in action and 425 wounded. The Communists lost nearly 1,000 fighters. The "Hill Fights," as the Marines came to know them, left the Americans in control of the high ground overlooking the remote base and denied the enemy observation posts from which they could direct artillery and

[259] Barry Nelson, "Helicopter Operations at Khe Sanh," *Marine Corps Gazette* 54, no. 5 (May 1969): 47.

[260] Shulimson et al., *The Defining Year, 1968*, 58; and Sturkey, *Bonnie-Sue*, 413–14.

rocket fire.[261] Starting in fall 1967, however, intelligence estimates suggested that as many as 40,000 North Vietnamese soldiers with heavy artillery encircled Khe Sanh.[262] Westmoreland believed that the enemy troops were surrounding the garrison in preparation for their real objective, an offensive that would overwhelm the RVN's two northern provinces.[263] Fresh paths hacked out of the jungle and data from air-dropped sensors warned the Marines that there was a large, well-equipped NVA force surrounding Khe Sanh. The threat of an enemy ambush effectively closed Route 9 by January 1968.[264] The entire 26th Marines, commanded by Colonel David E. Lownds, bolstered Khe Sanh's defenses, and additional CH-46s Sea Knights and Huey gunships arrived to support sweeps around the combat base.[265]

After months of preparation, North Vietnamese forces finally struck on the night of 21–22 January. Waves of enemy attacks hit the small, lightly defended hill outposts surrounding Khe Sanh. Bloody fighting prefaced the main NVA assault on the combat base itself, initiating the longest sustained enemy offensive in the northern provinces thus far in the war. Ringed by enemy artillery, rockets, and mortars, the Marines at Khe Sanh took vicious fire. A direct hit on the ammunition dump set alight more than 1,500 tons of ordnance, starting a chain of explosions. Enemy rounds also fell on the airfield, destroying two helicopters from HMM-262 parked in revetments, exploding barrels of aviation fuel, and ripping through the strip's steel planking surface.[266] The Americans responded with their own punishing fire. Artillery batteries created a wall of steel just beyond friendly lines. From the start of the conflict, air power was a key component of the American defense. Fixed-wing aircraft rocketed and bombed NVA firing positions while helicopters fed the fight with more Marines and supplies.[267]

The American effort to defend the combat base and the line of outposts that bowed around it required an impressive show of force. Although Boeing designed the B-52 Stratofortress strategic bomber for long-range Cold War missions, the aircraft provided tactical air support at Khe Sanh, shielding the besieged Marines and ARVN Rangers with a protective curtain of steel. Flying from bases in Guam, Thailand, and Okinawa, the U.S. Air Force bombers dropped nearly 60,000 tons of bombs on the hills around the base.[268] American airpower shook the ground daily, sending shockwaves that could be felt kilometers away. During Operation Niagara (January–March 1968), a torrent of bombs shattered the dense forests that concealed NVA soldiers. Detonations churned hilltops, pummeling the enemy entrenched in underground complexes with relentless concussions.[269]

An equally massive logistical effort kept Khe Sanh and its surrounding outposts in the fight. The Marines had built up a stockpile of 30 days of ammunition for all types of weapons, but the ammunition dump explosions destroyed 98 percent of that reserve.[270] Keeping the airstrip open was therefore essential to the base enduring the siege. This proved difficult as Fairchild C-123 Providers and Lockheed C-130 Hercules cargo aircraft made for easy targets for enemy small arms and shell fire while on the ground. For Khe Sanh to survive, aerial resupply had to continue regardless of the conditions. Cargo aircraft conducted nearly 500 supply drops via parachute. When they could land, aircrews rolled crates onto the runway from the back of still-moving aircraft to limit exposure time.[271]

Air Force and Marine aircraft delivered more than 14,000 tons of supplies during the siege through these varied means and methods. In addition to its normal operational responsibilities across I Corps supporting two reinforced Marine divisions and other ground forces, 1st Marine Aircraft Wing aircraft and personnel were stretched to the limits in early 1968.[272] The Marine air-ground team relied on rotary-wing aircraft for mobility, but static defenses such as those at Khe Sanh illustrated the importance of helicopters to the survival of units that were cut off.

Roughly 20 percent of the Marines in the area were located in the hill outposts, serving as the eyes and ears of the combat

[261] Andrew, *Hill Fights*, 55–59.
[262] Charles Peters, *Lyndon B. Johnson* (New York: Times Books, 2010), 141.
[263] Herbert Y. Schandler, *Lyndon Johnson and Vietnam: The Unmaking of a President* (Princeton, NJ: Princeton University Press, 1977), 86.
[264] Shulimson et al., *The Defining Year, 1968*, 61.
[265] Sturkey, *Bonnie-Sue*, 415.
[266] Shulimson et al., *The Defining Year, 1968*, 260.
[267] Bernard C. Nalty, *Air Power and the Fight for Khe Sanh* (Washington, DC: Office of Air Force History, 1986), 25.
[268] Shulimson et al., *The Defining Year, 1968*, 475.
[269] Shulimson et al., *The Defining Year, 1968*, 475.
[270] Shulimson et al., *The Defining Year, 1968*, 257–58.
[271] Nalty, *Air Power and the Fight for Khe Sanh*, 43–51.
[272] Shulimson et al., *The Defining Year, 1968*, 458.

Roy E. Moss Collection, Archives Branch, Marine Corps History Division

Marines load a CH-46 from HMM-262 (MAG-36) while a sling load is readied for hookup. With the ability to carry cargo internally and externally, Sea Knights were crucial lifelines to the isolated hill outposts surrounding Khe Sanh Combat Base.

base and the first line of defense.[273] Given the rough terrain, relative remoteness, and proximity to enemy positions, these satellite positions depended on helicopters for supplies, reinforcements, and to evacuate casualties. Crews flew day and night in wildly varying weather conditions to keep the hill outposts linked to outside help. MAG-36's relocation from Ky Ha to Phu Bai, 65 kilometers north of Da Nang, in October 1967 placed a large number of aircraft close to the DMZ. MAG-36 carried out the bulk of the work with helicopters operating out of Quang Tri and Dong Ha. HMM-262's CH-46 Sea Knights provided initial support at Khe Sanh, but HMM-364 assisted after the first squadron suffered heavy casualties in the frenetic fighting on the first day. MAG-16 rendered further aid with HMH-463. Taking on heavy-lift responsibilities, its CH-53 Sea Stallions flew more than 540 sorties and hauled nearly 820 tons of cargo in February in support of Khe Sanh.[274]

[273] Shore, *The Battle for Khe Sanh*, 23, 80.

[274] HMH-463 (MAG-16) ComdC, 1–29 February 1968 (7 March 1968), folder 92, U.S. Marine Corps History Division Vietnam War Documents Collection, item no. 1201105029, TTU Vietnam Archive, 4–7; and Sturkey, *Bonnie-Sue*, 424.

The timing and success of these missions were dictated by two issues: weather and enemy fire. Monsoon rain, low clouds, and fog in the mountainous terrain limited visibility and created nightmarish scenarios for pilots and crews. For all of February 1968, most bases in I Corps remained shrouded in a thick veil. Fog would roll in during the early evening, limiting visibility until burning off late the next morning.[275] The cloud base could be as low as 60 to 90 meters and the average visibility reduced to 3 kilometers.[276] Serene-looking clouds hid valleys and obscured mountains up to 900 meters tall. The weather forced rotary-wing crews to push on without the protection of tactical aircraft support. As a result, their unescorted helicopters suffered higher rates of hits in the air and on the ground.[277]

The poor weather forced pilots to fly solely with the aid of their onboard instruments. Rising up through "the soup," as pilots termed it, they would often not break into open skies until reaching an altitude of 1,800 meters. Despite the dangers, they developed methods to answer the outposts' calls for emergency resupply or casevacs. Major David L. Althoff, executive officer for HMM-262, professed to "know those hills like the back of my hand."[278] Flying up to the base of the clouds as helicopters neared the outpost, pilots would come to a hover and then use instruments to slowly rise into the cloudbank. The thick mist and thin air made level flight difficult. While pilots could sometimes catch glimpses of the ridgeline, ground troops usually used the sound of the rotors to guide the helicopters via radio communication. Even with such techniques, by mid-February the weather forced some of the outposts around Khe Sanh to hold out for three weeks without resupply because helicopters could not reach them.[279]

In addition to the weather, enemy fire was a persistent threat. North Vietnamese troops used the cover provided by the clouds to emplace heavy weapons on ridgelines and target Marine helicopters on their flight path to the hill out-

[275] HMM-262 (MAG-36) ComdC, 1–29 February 1968 (4 March 1968), folder 92, U.S. Marine Corps History Division Vietnam War Documents Collection, item no. 1201092039, TTU Vietnam Archive, 2.

[276] Headquarters, MAG-36, ComdC, February 1968 (18 March 1968), box 5, folder 5, VHPA Collection, item no. 2930505003, TTU Vietnam Archive, 6–9.

[277] HMM-262 (MAG-36) ComdC, 1–29 February 1968, 2.

[278] Nelson, "Helicopter Operations at Khe Sanh," 48.

[279] Nelson, "Helicopter Operations at Khe Sanh," 48–49.

Douglas Yeager Collection, Archives Branch, Marine Corps History Division

A CH-46 of HMM-364 delivering supplies in January 1968.

posts.[280] Marine crews endured an unprecedented amount of concentrated fire, including from numerous small arms and 12.7-millimeter antiaircraft guns. NVA gun crews also had the outposts targeted with mortars, making landing difficult for the helicopters. The first aircraft loss occurred on 20 January. "From then on," Major Althoff claimed, "it just turned into pure hell."[281] A dozen more CH-46s took extensive damage while parked on the ground at Khe Sanh. Any time Marine helicopter crews took to the air over Khe Sanh, they were flying through the most dangerous airspace in the Republic of Vietnam at the time. When Althoff and his fellow pilots approached a hill, the enemy would "have a round there by the time we touched down."[282]

By the end of February, enemy antiaircraft fire made it too dangerous for the Flying Tigers of HMM-262 to support the hill outposts, an experienced CH-46 unit headquartered at Quang Tri. The enemy shot down three helicopters supporting the remote forward bases on a single day. The squadron lost more than half its aircraft throughout February and siphoned more than a dozen pilots from HMM-364 to temporarily fill seats.[283] To cut down on their exposure time at the combat base, HMM-262 began flying out of Dong Ha, 30 kilometers to the east, with assistance from its sister squadron. On 28 February, Major Edwin G. Meixner, HMM-262's maintenance officer, carried reinforcements to Khe Sanh from the Quang Tri Air Facility on one such mission. Forced low due to bad weather, his Sea Knight took enemy fire from a 12.7-millimeter heavy machine gun, caught fire, and plummeted into a riverbed. All 23 Americans on board died in the crash, the worst single aircraft loss of the siege for the Marine Corps.[284]

Super Gaggle

Managing the antiaircraft fire and the larger logistical effort at Khe Sanh gave birth to a new strike system. Called the "Super Gaggle," it was an innovative, coordinated resupply mission that illustrated the full capabilities of the air-ground team. A group of planners at 1st MAW Headquarters devised the concept with the idea that every outpost required 16 tons of supplies per day.[285] In Operation Sierra on 24 February, eight CH-46s took off from Quang Tri and flew to Dong Ha. Each carried an external load of 3,000 pounds slung beneath the aircraft, which allowed the pilots to drop the cargo quickly if enemy fire became too intense. Support aircraft were already in the air, including two Huey command and control helicopters that could pick up any crews downed during the mission. Four Huey gunships from Quang Tri and a dozen Douglas

280 Shore, *The Battle for Khe Sanh*, 82.

281 Nelson, "Helicopter Operations at Khe Sanh," 47.

282 Nelson, "Helicopter Operations at Khe Sanh," 48.

283 John Prados and Ray W. Stubbe, *Valley of Decision: The Siege of Khe Sanh* (Boston, MA: Houghton Mifflin Company, 1991), 382.

284 HMM-262 (MAG-36) ComdC, 1–29 February 1968, 2.

285 Jones, *Last Stand at Khe Sanh*, 323–24; and Prados and Stubbe, *Valley of Decision*, 382.

A-4 Skyhawk single-seat light attack aircraft from MAG-12 at Chu Lai armed with a combination of napalm, tear gas canisters, rockets, bombs, and cannon provided suppressive fire in and around the landing zones. A Marine Lockheed Martin KC-130 tanker out of Da Nang was on station to refuel the aircraft. A tactical air controller on board a two-seater Douglas TA-4F Skyhawk coordinated the air-ground operation.[286]

The first operation so impressed 1st MAW's commanding general, Major General Norman J. Anderson, that he wrote Major General McCutcheon to report the "astonishing competence of the pilots and aircrewmen involved" who executed the mission quickly and smoothly. "Today was a small victory of that sort," he claimed, "and a most useful one." Due to the marginal weather and enemy activity, coordinated resupply operations would be required repeatedly in the coming weeks, but he was "confident that our great people can and will do what needs to be done in the critical battle at Khe Sanh."[287]

Despite the Super Gaggle's chaotic appearance, it was a well-choreographed procedure. According to Lieutenant Colonel Carey, one of the planners behind the concept, success "was predicated on timing, coordination, and oftentimes luck," which meant "the ability to guess whether the weather would hold long enough to complete an effort once it got underway."[288] The squadron that flew the majority of the missions, HMM-262, reported that it required "much skill and fortitude."[289] All pilots observed prescribed takeoff times so that the various elements arrived over the area at the precise moment. The command and control UH-1Es would already be over Khe Sanh when the fixed-wing aircraft arrived from Chu Lai. By that point, the CH-46s were en route to their objective from Dong Ha.[290]

Early in the siege, pilots typically traveled up Route 9 at 900 meters and entered the area from the south. The enemy countered by emplacing guns to cover this approach. As a result, Marine helicopter pilots chose a northern route through the valleys at 1,500 meters until over the friendly lines, then initiated a steep spiral descent.[291] As the CH-46 Sea Knights neared their destinations, a pair of A-4 Skyhawks dropped tear gas canisters onto enemy antiaircraft positions. With the helicopters on their final approach, only 30–40 seconds from the landing zone, another pair of A-4s laid down a smoke screen on either side of the flight path to obscure it from enemy view. Just as the heavily laden Sea Knights approached their target, four Skyhawks and Huey gunships dove on the landing zone, unleashing bombs, rockets, and cannon fire to force the enemy to take cover. Timing was key to the operation, but so was the effectiveness of this fire suppression—once committed, the cargo helicopter pilots had no alternative but to press on, comforted slightly by the UH-1Es following close behind that would attempt to rescue them if shot down.[292]

Using these new methods, the Marines lost only two Sea Knights in March, delivering 80,000 pounds of cargo each day to the hill positions. The efficiency of the missions increased when helicopter formations split into two after dropping their sling loads. One-half made another trip into the hills to unload internal cargo or troop reinforcements while the other landed at the Khe Sanh combat base to pick up casualties and other passengers.[293] If the weather permitted, the teams could execute up to four Super Gaggles from Dong Ha into the valley per day.[294] The operations lifted morale among ground troops, a turning point for Marines enduring the siege in the hill outposts. With A-4s and UH-1E gunships suppressing enemy fire, Marines felt safer leaving their positions to retrieve supplies. "If it weren't for the Gaggle," Captain William H. Dabney, commander of Company I, 3d Battalion, 26th Marines, claimed, "most of us probably wouldn't be here today."[295]

As the weather improved, MAG-36 and MAG-16 could attempt to keep up with the additional support required by the defenders to maintain normal operations. The 26th Marines had five battalions in place at the end of January, requiring 185 tons of supplies per day, up from 60 tons in mid-January.[296] Ammunition always took priority in the aerial resupplies. Troops might not have enjoyed an inexhaustible

[286] Shulimson et al., *The Defining Year, 1968*, 483–85; Shore, *The Battle for Khe Sanh*, 84–86; and Jones, *Last Stand at Khe Sanh*, 200–201.
[287] Letter from MajGen Norman J. Anderson to MajGen Keith B. McCutcheon, 25 February 1968, box 20, folder 5, Gen Keith B. McCutcheon Papers, HD Archive, 1–2.
[288] Shore, *The Battle for Khe Sanh*, 84.
[289] HMM-262 (MAG-36) ComdC, 1–29 February 1968, 2.
[290] Althoff and Nelson, "Helicopter Operations at Khe Sanh," 48.
[291] Jones, *Last Stand at Khe Sanh*, 230.
[292] Shore, *The Battle for Khe Sanh*, 86.
[293] Nelson, "Helicopter Operations at Khe Sanh," 48.
[294] Shulimson et al., *The Defining Year, 1968*, 484–85.
[295] Shore, *The Battle for Khe Sanh*, 89.
[296] This included the three battalions of the 26th Marines; 1st Battalion, 9th Marines; and the 37th ARVN Ranger Battalion.

Jonathan F. Abel Collection, Archives Branch, Marine Corps History Division

At Marble Mountain, a VMO-2 gunship crew chief signs paperwork after refueling the aircraft.

daily surplus, but they never faced desperate shortages of essentials, and they never went hungry. If weather prevented flights, disciplined consumption of food and water at the base and the hill outposts ensured adequate amounts for all.[297] In total, between November 1967 and March 1968, Marine helicopters flew 9,100 sorties, moved 14,500 passengers, and delivered 4,600 tons of materiel in support of the Marine positions at Khe Sanh.[298]

Relief and reinforcement of Khe Sanh came in April with Operation Pegasus, the largest effort by III MAF yet. Major General John J. Tolson III—one of the U.S. Army's earliest proponents of helimobile forces—commanded more than just his own 1st Cavalry Division during Pegasus. Elements from the ARVN, U.S. Army, and Marine Corps (including Colonel Lowland's 26th Marines) totaling 30,000 troops were at his disposal. On 1 April, the relief force began air assaulting toward the base while the encircled Marines left their static positions and attacked. By 8 April, the forces linked up and the 77-day siege of Khe Sanh finally ended.[299]

The Tet Offensive

Soon after the first attack on Khe Sanh and the hill outposts, enemy forces launched coordinated attacks on major population centers across the Republic of Vietnam during the Vietnamese holiday of Tet. Beginning on the night of 31 January

[297] Shore, *The Battle for Khe Sanh*, 90.

[298] Prados, *Valley of Decision*, 383.

[299] LtGen John J. Tolson, USA, *Airmobility, 1961–1971*, Vietnam Studies (Washington, DC: Department of the Army, 1999), 169–77; and Shore, *The Battle for Khe Sanh*, 132–44.

1ST MAW HELICOPTER UNITS, APRIL 1968

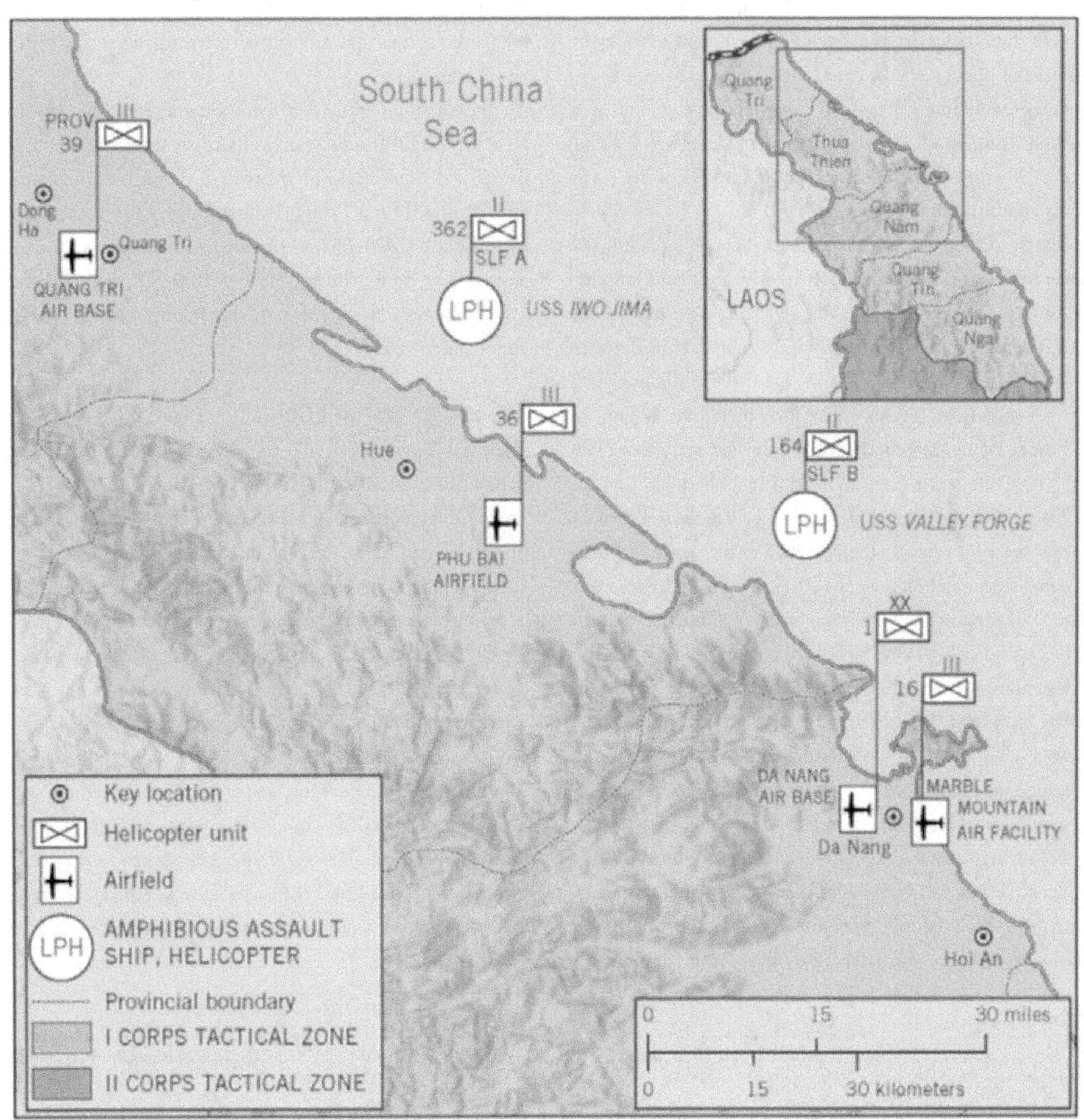

Map courtesy of Pete McPhail, adapted by MCUP

1968, the NVA targeted American and South Vietnamese military installations while the Viet Cong attacked civilian and military command and control centers in urban areas.

The enemy's intent behind the general offensive and popular uprising was to destabilize the South Vietnamese government and trigger rebellions.[300] The Communists suffered a brutal tactical defeat as American and ARVN units anni-

300 Pierre Asselin, *Vietnam's American War: A History* (New York: Cambridge University Press, 2018), 152–53.

hilated the Viet Cong, reducing the NLF's ability to field an effective force for the next two years. Nonetheless, the operation achieved a political victory. The attacks eroded Vietnamese confidence in the Saigon government's ability to protect the population. In the United States, Americans saw footage—including Viet Cong fighters inside the U.S. embassy compound in Saigon—that made them question General Westmoreland and President Johnson's positive statements about the state of the war.[301]

The Tet Offensive forced Marine helicopter squadrons to divide their forces between supplying Khe Sanh and supporting multiple operations throughout I Corps, particularly in the battle for Vietnam's former imperial capital, Hue. Between 31 January and 2 March, 3 Marine infantry battalions, 2 U.S. Army brigades, and 11 ARVN infantry battalions fought one of the longest and bloodiest battles of the war against an NVA and Viet Cong strike force equivalent to 14 battalions.[302]

Enemy sappers blew the An Cuu bridge on 4 February, closing the land route to the city. As a result, boats and helicopters became the only means of reaching friendly forces in Hue.[303] Marine helicopters brought in reinforcements as the battle expanded and rushed wounded to field hospitals. MAG-36 aircraft alone evacuated nearly 1,200 casualties from Hue during February.[304] Operating in an urban environment put crews in close proximity to entrenched NVA and Viet Cong. The same month, 140 MAG-36 aircraft took hits, the majority while supporting Operation Hue City.[305]

Following the fall of the Citadel, an enemy bastion within the city, ARVN and U.S. forces cleared the remaining resistance and declared the operation complete by 2 March. Marine helicopters ultimately flew 500 tons of supplies into Hue in addition to the 400 tons that Navy landing craft transported to shore.[306] Despite persistently poor weather, 1st Marine Aircraft Wing squadrons managed 1,096 passenger and cargo sorties and 189 casualty evacuation sorties during the operation.[307]

The losses for 1st MAW were testament to the punishing fight for the air-ground team in I Corps during the first phase of the Tet Offensive. In February and March, the wing lost 10 CH-46s, 3 CH-53s, 7 UH-1s, and 5 UH-34s.[308] In the same time frame, HMM-262, flying many of the sorties to the hills around Khe Sanh, suffered 43 casualties. Of those, 21 were killed in action. At the end of March, only 11 of its aircraft commanders remained.[309]

The Larger War in I Corps

The expanding war in 1967–68 reinforced the interconnected nature of the Marine air-ground team. The U.S. Army's Task Force Oregon arrived in southern I Corps in April 1967 to fill the vacuum left by Marine units that moved north to face enemy regulars crossing into the Republic of Vietnam.[310] By September, its three brigades consolidated into the 23d Infantry Division (Americal) with its own substantial organic helicopter support.[311] As a result, III MAF was able to move some forces north to operate around Da Nang and in the mountains of Quang Tri Province.[312]

The 3d Marine Division was mostly fixed in remote positions near the DMZ to stop NVA cross-border incursions.[313] Ground operations in such remote areas strained the available rotary-wing capabilities. The main issue was distance. MAG-16's six squadrons were based out of Da Nang, more than 160

[301] Ngo Vinh Long, "The Tet Offensive and Its Aftermath," in *The American War in Vietnam*, ed. Jayne Werner and David Hunt (Ithaca, NY: Southeast Asia Program, Cornell University Press, 1993), 23–45; and Chester J. Pach Jr., "The War on Television: TV News, the Johnson Administration, and Vietnam," in *A Companion to the Vietnam War*, ed. Marilyn B. Young and Robert Buzzanco (Malden, MA: Blackwell Publishers, 2002), 450–69.

[302] Col Richard D. Camp Jr., USMC (Ret), *Death in the Imperial City: U.S. Marines in the Battle for Hue, 31 January to 2 March 1968*, Marines in the Vietnam War Commemorative Series (Quantico, VA: Marine Corps History Division, 2018), 4–8.

[303] Shulimson et al., *The Defining Year, 1968*, 185.

[304] MAG-36 ComdC, 1 February 1968–29 February 1968 (18 March 1968), box 04, folder 49, VHPA Collection, item no 2930449016, TTU Vietnam Archive, 19.

[305] MAG-36 ComdC, 1 February 1968–29 February 1968, 19.

[306] Shulimson et al., *The Defining Year, 1968*, 216.

[307] Shulimson et al., *The Defining Year, 1968*, 219; and 1st MAW ComdC, February 1968 (7 April 1968), folder 68, U.S. Marine Corps History Division, Vietnam War Documents Collection, item no. 1201068022, TTU Vietnam Archive, 2–3.

[308] 1st MAW ComdC, February 1968, 2–3; and 1st MAW ComdC, March 1968, folder 68, U.S. Marine Corps History Division Vietnam War Documents Collection, item no. 1201068023, TTU Vietnam Archive, 2–4.

[309] HMM-262 (MAG-36) ComdC, 1–31 March 1968 (4 April 1968), folder 92, U.S. Marine Corps History Division Vietnam War Documents Collection, item no. 1201092040, TTU Vietnam Archive.

[310] Shulimson et al., *The Defining Year, 1968*, 11.

[311] An aviation battalion was organic to each U.S. Army infantry division in the Vietnam War era.

[312] Shulimson et al., *The Defining Year, 1968*, 11–12, 84.

[313] Shulimson et al., *The Defining Year, 1968*, 8, 11.

TABLE 2. 1ST MAW HELICOPTER UNITS AND HELICOPTERS IN SOUTHEAST ASIA, APRIL 1968

MAG-16 Marble Mountain Air Facility		MAG-36 Phu Bai Airfield		PROVMAG-39 Quang Tri Combat Base		SLF ALPHA USS *Iwo Jima*		SLF BRAVO USS *Valley Forge*	
Unit	Aircraft number/type	Unit	Aircraft number/type	Unit	Aircraft number/type	Unit	Aircraft number/type	Unit	Aircraft number/type
VMO-2	11—UH-1E	HMM-165	19—CH-46A	VMO-6	22—UH-1E	HMM-362	20—UH-34D	HMM-164	20—CH-46A
HMM-265	17—UH-34D	HMM-363	23—UH-34D	HMM-163	21—UH-34D				
HML-167	17—UH-34D	HMM-364	18—CH-46D	HMM-262	24—CH-46A				
HMM-361	21—UH-34D	HML-367	18—UH-1E						
HMM-463	27—CH-53A								

Source: Report, Marine Corps Command Center, "Status of Fleet Marine Forces," 30 April 1968, Status of Forces file, Reference Branch Collection, Archives Branch, Marine Corps History Division, Quantico, VA.

kilometers from the DMZ. MAG-36's five squadrons at Phu Bai were 110 kilometers away. To decrease response time and strengthen the air-ground team, the Marines created a temporary aircraft group closer to the fighting. Provisional Marine Aircraft Group 39 (ProvMAG-39) came together in April 1968 from three MAG-36 units already operating near the provincial capital of Quang Tri, about 65 kilometers northwest of Phu Bai. Despite the provisional character of the new aircraft group, it gave III MAF a semipermanent helimobile capability only 50 kilometers from the DMZ.[314]

ProvMAG-39 and the other Marine aircraft groups assisted ground elements in repelling yet another enemy nationwide attack that began on 5 May 1968. While bloodied in the Tet Offensive, the NVA still possessed combat power. The May offensive had the limited objectives of inflicting American and South Vietnamese casualties and agitating urban areas. A month of heavy fighting cost the enemy 30,000 casualties with little return. Allied air and ground forces drove main force elements back to their remote base areas and cross-border sanctuaries.[315]

The Khe Sanh Combat Base closed on 5 July 1968. Ground units were out of their static positions and continuing the battle in a new form by then, as Marine, Army, and ARVN units were on the offensive across I Corps.[316] Driving into remote enemy base areas with greater frequency after Tet, the Marines became increasingly dependent on the added mobility of rotary-wing support. In the heavy assault operations against North Vietnamese divisions, Marine helicopters transported 50,000 troops and 6,000 tons of cargo each month on average, a 25 percent increase in passengers and 200 percent rise in supplies compared to the end of 1965.[317] Depleted and demoralized NVA forces needed rest and refitting by the end of the year and sought the relative safety of the A Shau Valley. The pause provided U.S. and South Vietnamese forces time to devise a campaign plan for the coming year.[318]

[314] Report, Marine Corps Command Center, "Status of Fleet Marine Forces," 31 March 1968, Status of Forces file, Reference Branch Collection, HD Archive.

[315] Cosmas, *MACV: The Joint Command in the Years of Escalation, 1962–1967*, 111–12.

[316] Shore, *The Battle for Khe Sanh*, 149–51.

[317] McCutcheon, "Marine Aviation in Vietnam," 186.

[318] Smith, *High Mobility and Standdown, 1969*, 26.

Jonathan F. Abel Collection, Archives Branch, Marine Corps History Division

With ProvMAG-39 operating out of Quang Tri, sweeps of northern I Corps like this three-squadron lift during late August 1968 were possible.

Marine Helicopters in 1969

Beginning in mid-1968, the 3d Marine Division commander, Major General Raymond G. Davis, sought to abandon the emphasis on using fixed positions to control territory. He had seen "floods of helicopters" up close as a deputy to U.S. Army lieutenant General William B. Rosson, commander of the Provisional Corps, Vietnam, in northern I Corps.[319] These experiences convinced Davis of the need for the Marine Corps to employ a version of the Army's air assault operational approach in I Corps that used the air-ground team to best effect. He argued that the 1st Cavalry Division's relief of Khe Sanh "demonstrated the decisiveness of high mobility operations" and the effectiveness of a heavy reliance on helicopters.[320] He believed that the Marines needed to "get out of those fixed positions, to get mobile and go out to destroy the enemy on our terms," rather than enduring the enemy's large guns and regular attacks on firebases.[321]

Davis published these thoughts in September 1968 in a *Marine Corps Gazette* piece that he coauthored with his aide, Captain Richard D. Camp. Their thesis gave a nod to the Army's airmobility concept that stressed speed, mobility, flexibility, and firepower. At its heart, Davis and Camp's article argued that U.S. Army air assault techniques would make Marine forces much more effective in I Corps.[322]

The initial test of the concept that Davis dubbed "high mobility" occurred shortly after he took command of 3d Marine Division in May 1968. High mobility relied on unit cohesion, support, and maneuverability. In practice, this meant heliborne assaults to hilltops, where artillery units would estab-

[319] Gen Raymond G. Davis, interview with Benis M. Frank, 2 February 1977, transcript, Marine Corps Oral History Collection, 16–17, hereafter Davis interview.

[320] Davis interview, 17.

[321] Davis interview, 17; Raymond G. Davis, *The Story of Ray Davis* (Fuquay-Varina, NC: Research Triangle Publishing, 1995), 192; and Smith, *High Mobility and Standdown, 1969*, 16.

[322] MajGen R. G. Davis and Capt R. D. Camp, "Marines in Assault by Helicopter," *Marine Corps Gazette* 52, no. 9 (September 1968): 22–28.

Marine Light Helicopter (HML) Squadron

Defense Department (Marine Corps) A192655

New technology triggered organizational changes for III Marine Amphibious Force and Marine Aviation. The Corps' new North American Rockwell OV-10A Bronco fixed-wing aircraft were slated to arrive at Marine Observation Squadrons (VMO) in 1968. Its light attack and observation capabilities meant the airplane could assume those roles from the overstretched UH-1Es. Rather than reducing the number of light helicopters in-country, however, the Marine Corps moved the extra Hueys into a new type of squadron that General McCutcheon devised as a temporary wartime expedient: the Marine Light Helicopter Squadron. Equipped as gunless "slick" variants—so-called for their outward appearance shorn of protruding weapons—HML UH-1Es flew utility and administrative tasks. On 15 March 1968, the Marine Corps began organizing three new units, starting with HML-267 at Pendleton, California. HML-368 formed a week later at Phu Bai, and HML-167 at Marble Mountain soon after. This reorganization saw the end of VMO-3 and -5, as their personnel and aircraft joined the new HMLs.[1]

[1] LtCol William R. Fails, USMC, *Marines and Helicopters, 1962–1973* (Washington, DC: History and Museums Division, Headquarters, U.S. Marine Corps, 1978), 113; and Jack Shulimson et al., *U.S. Marines in Vietnam: The Defining Year, 1968* (Washington, DC: History and Museums Division, Headquarters, U.S. Marine Corps, 1997), 519–21.

lish fire support bases to provide a protective fan for infantry units operating below. Throughout the summer and fall of 1968, the regiments of the 3d Marine Division perfected the concept in areas near the Laotian border where no other Marine or ARVN units had operated before, proving that it was applicable to the mountains of western I Corps.

From base areas in Quang Tri and Thua Thien Provinces that straddled the Laotian border, the NVA supplied Viet Cong operations deeper inside South Vietnam. Enemy troops chose as their base area a secluded and mountainous area in which no major American or South Vietnamese unit had operated. From the Da Krong Valley, a 40-kilometer-long rolling valley with ridgelines that climbed to 900 meters, the NVA staged troops and materiel for movement southeast to the A Shau Valley, a natural avenue of invasion that the NVA had used for four years to supply operations against the coastal population and urban centers like Hue and Da Nang.[323]

The first in a series of 3d Marine Division operations that swept the border in search of enemy base areas was Operation Dawson River, on 28 November. A thorough search of the area between Laos and the now-abandoned Khe Sanh Combat Base by Marines between November and January 1969 did not turn up much, but it did reveal that if the enemy was not in the western Quang Tri, they were certainly in the Da Krong and A Shau valleys.[324]

At the beginning of January 1969, American aircraft began taking enemy small arms and antiaircraft fire along the road network that stretched from Laos into the A Shau, called Base Area 611. Aerial reconnaissance spotted freshly laid wires for a sophisticated communication network. NVA engineer units opened up infiltration routes from the Ho Chi Minh Trail in Laos to both valleys. As many as 1,000 trucks per day traveled parallel to the border on Route 922 in Laos. With a fragmented patchwork of intelligence and the lessons of the 1968 Tet Offensive, the 3d Marine Division leadership perceived that the enemy was preparing once again to use the Tet holiday to pressure the population centers in the Republic of Vietnam.[325]

In response, the 3d Marine Division ordered the 9th Marines to launch what became Operation Dewey Canyon on 22 January with the objective of destroying the enemy's ability to fight and refuse access to the populated coastal lowlands. The Marines would do so by stopping Communist infiltration into I Corps through the A Shau and destroying the logistical base areas. The NVA and Viet Cong had underground storage areas, distribution centers, command posts, bivouac areas, artillery positions, and engineer equipment in the region.[326] Destroying these would ostensibly cripple their operations from Quang Tri to Da Nang and neutralize the threat to I Corps. The operation targeted the southern Da Krong and the mouth of the A Shau, respectively falling within the southwestern region of Quang Tri and the western area of Thua Thien Province.[327]

Planners devised Dewey Canyon as a three-phase operation. Three infantry battalions would helilift into the Da Krong from Vandegrift Combat Base and establish hilltop fire support bases. From there, the battalions would sweep down the valley and position themselves at the Da Krong River for a regimental attack. In the final phase, the regiment would assault into Base Area 611. The ultimate objectives were the twin peaks of Hill 1224 (Tam Boi) and Hill 1228 (Tiger Mountain) that divided the two valleys and overlooked the approaches into the A Shau. Dewey Canyon was an ambitious, aggressive thrust into enemy-dominated territory that depended heavily upon helicopter mobility. Marine aircrews would be traversing dangerous terrain in poor weather and entering an area the North Vietnamese considered a defendable sanctuary.[328]

With troops operating dozens of kilometers beyond permanent support bases, well out of range for naval gunfire, and nowhere close to road networks on which supplies and reinforcements could arrive, the operation's success was reliant upon the mobility that helicopters provided. Rotary-wing aircraft allowed the Marines and ARVN to build up rapidly in

[323] Headquarters, Pacific Air Forces, "A Shau Valley Campaign, December 1968–May 1969," Contemporary Historical Examination of Current Operations (CHECO) Reports of Southeast Asia, 1961–1975, folder 1, Bud Harton Collection, item no. 168300010935, TTU Vietnam Archive, 5; Gordon M. Davis, "Dewey Canyon: All Weather Classic," *Marine Corps Gazette* 53, no. 7 (July 1969): 32–40; and Maj Allan C. Bevilacqua, "Operation Dewey Canyon: Cleaning Up the A Shau Valley," *Leatherneck* 97, no. 4 (April 2014): 25–26.

[324] Tom Bartlett, "Operation Dewey Canyon," *Leatherneck* 77, no. 2 (February 1994): 34.

[325] Seth A. Givens, *On Our Terms: Marines in Operation Dewey Canyon, 22 January to 18 March 1969*, Marines in the Vietnam War Commemorative Series (Quantico, VA: Marine Corps History Division, 2021), 1–2.

[326] Davis, "Dewey Canyon," 34.

[327] Givens, *On Our Terms*, 19–23.

[328] Givens, *On Our Terms*, 21.

DA KRONG VALLEY

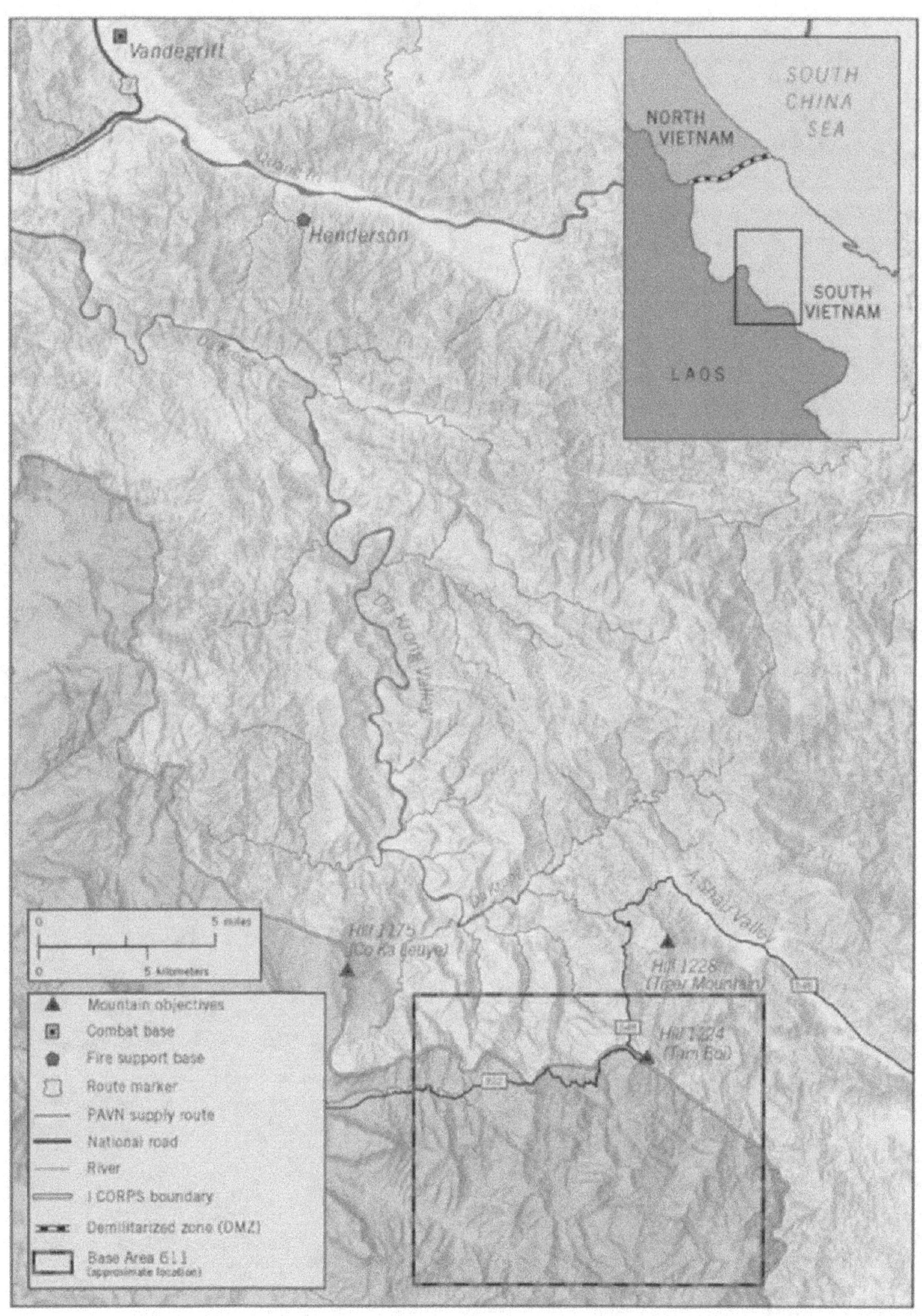

Map courtesy of Pete McPhail, adapted by MCUP

Sikorsky CH-53A Sea Stallion

By the early 1960s, gas turbine-powered helicopters were entering the inventories of all U.S. military branches, offering more favorable power-to-weight ratios than piston engines. While the Bell UH-1E filled a utility role and the Boeing-Vertol CH-46 Sea Knight handled the medium-lift role, the Marine Corps lacked a replacement for the aging, piston-powered Sikorsky HR2S-1/CH-37C heavy-lift helicopter.

Responding to the design requirements for a turbine-powered, heavy-lift aircraft with a rear ramp, the Marine Corps' 1962 Heavy Helicopter Experimental (HHX) design competition pitted Boeing-Vertol's modified CH-47 Chinook against Sikorsky's challenger, designated the S-65. The Sikorsky's transmission system was updated from the CH-37C and benefited from a decade of operational experience and data. Two General Electric T64-GE-6 turboshaft engines mounted high on either side of the fuselage powered the large single-rotor system. In September 1962, the Department of Defense announced that S-65 was the winner.

The Fleet Marine Force received the first production versions in 1966, now designated the CH-53A Sea Stallion. A detachment of four arrived in Vietnam on 8 January 1967, just as the handful of CH-37s in-country reached the end of their service life. Within months, there were three times the number of CH-53s operating in Vietnam as the aircraft they replaced, compiling more than 13,000 flight hours in the first year.

By size, range, power, and capability, the "Super Bird," as some Marines came to call it, was close to the archetypal helicopter that early vertical envelopment planners had in mind when developing the concept as part of the air-ground team. The heavy-lift capability of the Sea Stallion allowed it to set Marine records in cargo and personnel moved. With enough power to carry an internal cargo of four tons or six tons externally, the CH-53A was particularly useful returning disabled

Robert L. Drieslein Collection, Archives Branch, Marine Corps History Division

UH-34Ds and CH-46s to maintenance facilities from the field. Hydraulically boosted controls, good stability, a range of up to 320 kilometers, a relatively quick cruising speed for its size, and an all-weather capability found favor among pilots. Improved variants over the years have kept the CH-53 in the Marine inventory to present day.[1]

[1] LtCol William R. Fails, USMC, *Marines and Helicopters, 1962–1973* (Washington, DC: History and Museums Division, Headquarters, U.S. Marine Corps, 1978), 59–60; *USMC/Vietnam Helicopter Association: Pop A Smoke* (Paducah, KY: Turner Publishing, 2001), 29; and Helmet E. Dost, *Marine Corps and Army Helicopter Employment and Attrition Statistics for Southeast Asia Operations from October 1965 through December 1971*, vol. 2, Study 1008 (Arlington, VA: Center for Naval Analyses, 1972), 43–44.

Defense Department (Marine Corps) 2-2591-68

A CH-53 lifts a sling load from the stockpiled supplies at Vandegrift Combat Base in October 1968 while a CH-46 flares for landing. CH-53s were an integral part of MajGen Raymond Davis's high mobility approach throughout Dewey Canyon.

the area, developing a presence that would have taken months by ground. Helicopters were most important in the assault phase, where battalions launched from Vandegrift Combat Base into the Da Krong and then continued to push south into the A Shau. Not only would the aircraft allow them to bypass punishing terrain, but they enabled the Marines to mass both personnel and supplies within hours. Engineering units were to use construction equipment and chainsaws to carve landing zones out of the jungle.[329]

[329] Davis, "Dewey Canyon: All Weather Classic," 33–36.

For eight weeks, Marine rotorcraft funneled into western I Corps to support the operation. Most came from a half dozen squadrons belonging to MAG-16.[330] Sea Knights took up the largest share of the burden. The updated CH-46Ds—fitted with more powerful turboshaft engines and structural changes from Boeing-Vertol—could lift an entire platoon to the mountaintop landing zones. Marine UH-1E Hueys were also kept busy in the operation, ferrying supplies and escorting

[330] Smith, *High Mobility and Standdown, 1969*, 220; and MAG-16 ComdC, 1–28 February 1969, HD Archive.

transports, while UH-34D Seahorses flew casevac missions. These aircraft were key to establishing and supporting firebases that acted as stepping-stones for sequential strikes farther into the valley, inserting troops, and supplying the operation.[331]

Dewey Canyon also relied on the Marine Corps CH-53A Sea Stallions, which could lift the bulky heavy equipment needed to convert jungle-covered mountaintops into installations.[332] Fire support bases not only housed the command posts for the operation but were also artillery platforms. CH-53s brought in heavy guns, which provided overlapping eight-kilometer fire zones for the infantry units maneuvering deeper into the valley. Starting in mid-January, units reopened three former fire support bases in the northern Da Krong Valley: Henderson, Tun Tavern, and Shiloh. From these bases, the Marines quickly built additional fire support bases: Razor, Erskine, and Cunningham farther south. As they moved beyond the range of their fire support, the air-ground team would pick up and start the leapfrog process of fire support bases again.[333]

As with the defense of Khe Sanh the year before, weather proved to be the major limiting factor to what rotary-wing units could accomplish. Poor visibility and low cloud ceilings limited flight times by more than one-half and constricted operational alternatives. Overcast skies, steady drizzle, dense fog, and low-hanging clouds enveloped the hills and mountains in the Da Krong and A Shau valleys. Fixed-wing close-air support was grounded for days at a time, and the fire support bases were cut off from resupply, reinforcement, and casevac aircraft operating from Vandegrift Combat Base some 40 kilometers away. However, sudden breaks in the weather made air operations possible. With a large buildup of supplies and personnel waiting to go in, helicopter crews took to the air whenever possible with reinforcements and sling loads of food, water, ammunition, and other supplies.[334]

Dewey Canyon represented the largest single sustained Marine rotary-wing effort of the war. Organic aviation assets from the U.S. Army's 101st Airborne Division gave additional assistance to 1st MAW. Boeing-Vertol CH-47 Chinooks and Sikorsky CH-54 Tarhe heavy-lift helicopters were ideal for constructing, supplying, and displacing the fire support bases and their 105mm and 155mm howitzers. In addition, Army cavalry observation and attack helicopters flew reconnaissance missions that provided the Marines and ARVN protection on their flanks and rear areas.[335]

During the 56 days of Operation Dewey Canyon, helicopters from the 1st MAW flew approximately 14,300 sorties. To improve time management, the wing's liaison officer attached to 3d Marine Division to coordinate air operations "on the spot."[336] By 18 March, Marine rotorcraft totaled nearly 5,000 hours in the air supporting Dewey Canyon. Helicopters conducted nearly 50 company-size or larger troop lifts during the operation, carrying more than 20,200 passengers. The exceptional mobility that heavy-lift helicopters provided underpinned the operational approach of leapfrogging firebases, allowing the Marines to displace 22 artillery batteries as well as move 7.2 million pounds of cargo.[337]

In large part because of helicopter mobility, USMACV considered the strike into the Da Krong and A Shau a success, as it immediately interrupted the enemy's ability to target military and civilian populations to the east. In the near term, Dewey Canyon paralyzed North Vietnamese supply lines into I Corps and made sizeable enemy offensives impossible during the following months. The 9th Marines captured or destroyed 500 tons of arms and munitions, more than 1,200 individual weapons, 8 122mm field guns, 73 antiaircraft guns, and 92 trucks, while claiming 1,617 enemy killed. Meeting stiff resistance from well-supplied and trained NVA units, the Marines lost 130 killed in action and another 920 wounded.[338] Of the performance, General Stilwell reported to General Creighton W. Abrams Jr., U.S. Army, who took command of USMACV

---

[331] Headquarters, 9th Marines to Headquarters, 3d Marines, "Combat Operation After Action Report," 8 April 1969, box 9, folder 14, Vietnam War Collection, HD Archive, 7.

[332] Headquarters, 9th Marines to Headquarters, 3d Marines, "Combat Operation After Action Report," 8 April 1969, 7.

[333] Bevilacqua, "Cleaning Up the A Shau Valley," 28.

[334] Charles D. Melson, "Dewey Canyon, Thirty Years Later," *Fortitudine* 28, no. 2 (1999): 4–5; and Col Robert H. Barrow, interview with SSgt Willis S. Bernard Jr., 8 April 1969, Marine Corps Oral History Collection, HD Archive.

[335] Givens, *On Our Terms*, 32–33.

[336] As quoted in *USMC/Vietnam Helicopter Association: Pop a Smoke*, 19.

[337] 1st MAW ComdC, January 1969 (2 March 1969), folder 68, U.S. Marine Corps History Division Vietnam War Documents Collection, item no. 1201068033, TTU Vietnam Archive, 5; 1st MAW ComdC, February 1969 (29 March 1969), folder 68, U.S. Marine Corps History Division Vietnam War Documents Collection, item no. 1201068034, TTU Vietnam Archive, 13; and 1st MAW ComdC, March 1969 (7 May 1969), folder 68, U.S. Marine Corps History Division Vietnam War Documents Collection, item no. 1201068035, TTU Vietnam Archive, 12.

[338] Smith, *High Mobility and Standdown, 1969*, 50.

Jonathan F. Abel Collection, Archives Branch, Marine Corps History Division

Rain, low clouds, and dense fog limited helicopter operations during Operation Dewey Canyon. Helicopter crews took advantage of any suitable breaks in the weather to deliver much-needed supplies.

from Westmoreland on 10 June 1968, that as an operation "it may be unparalleled."[339]

Withdrawal, 1969–71

After taking office in January 1969, President Richard M. Nixon began to reduce U.S. combat forces in Southeast Asia. As part of the administration's Vietnamization plan, the United States would limit its direct involvement in combat operations in favor of South Vietnamese forces.[340] The Joint Chiefs of Staff worked on plans to reduce the number of U.S. personnel in Vietnam through successive redeployments, focusing initially on aviation and support units. The first withdrawal of Marines from I Corps began in June 1969, a reduction of more than 26,800 that included 3d Marine Division. A handful of 1st MAW squadrons and fixed-wing units made up some of the early departures. The Marble Mountain-based HMM-165 from MAG-16 was the first Marine rotary-wing unit to redeploy, departing for Okinawa on 14 August with its Sea Knights on board *Valley Forge* (LPH 8). HMH-462 of MAG-36 followed on 20 October.[341]

As Vietnamization took hold, Marine helicopter assets in-country steadily dwindled. HMM-362 flew its final missions on 15 August. The "Ugly Angels" were the first Shufly Marines to arrive in Vietnam in April 1962, beginning the lengthy operational history of Marine helicopters in Southeast Asia. HMM-362 was also the last UH-34D Seahorse squadron in Vietnam, exchanging the reliable machines for CH-53 Sea

[339] As quoted in Smith, *High Mobility and Standdown, 1969*, 51.

[340] Gregory A. Daddis, *Withdrawal: Reassessing America's Final Years in Vietnam* (New York: Oxford University Press, 2017), 45–75.

[341] *USMC/Vietnam Helicopter Association: Pop a Smoke*, 83; Smith, *High Mobility and Standdown*, 1969, 343–44, 356; and Report, Marine Corps Command Center, "Status of Fleet Marine Forces," 20 May 1969, Status of Forces file, Reference Branch Collection, HD Archive.

Jonathan F. Abel Collection, Archives Branch, Marine Corps History Division

A flight of CH-46s from HMM-165 pass over their MAG-16 base at Marble Mountain for a final time en route to boarding ships for Okinawa, the first major 1st MAW unit to depart Vietnam as part of the drawdown.

Stallions once it arrived in Japan and redesignated as a Marine heavy helicopter (HMH) squadron.[342]

With 3d Marine Division leaving Vietnam, ProvMAG-39 was no longer needed in northern I Corps. As Colonel Eugene R. Brady, former squadron commander of HMM-364, observed, "It was born there, lived there, and as an old soldier, it just faded away."[343] VMO-6 departed the Republic of Vietnam for Okinawa on 12 October 1969. Administrative and operational control of HMM-161 and HMM-262 transferred to MAG-16 by 16 October. Meanwhile, the squadron's headquarters relocated to Phu Bai and its commanding officer assumed command of MAG-36.[344] That group also exited Vietnam soon after, leaving for Okinawa on 7 November 1969, almost four years after it first arrived.[345] MAG-16, the first Marine helicopter group to arrive in Vietnam, remained behind, adding to an impressive history of combat accomplishments.[346]

By early 1970, large-scale combat for III MAF became increasingly uncommon. The collapse of the enemy's logistical networks in 1968 and 1969 limited the NVA's ability to conduct large attacks. As a result, ambushes and skirmishes replaced battalion- or regiment-size operations. For the Marines, gone were the large ground actions that typified the previous two years as the operational focus narrowed to the area around Da Nang. Throughout the Republic of Vietnam in 1970, ARVN units assumed a larger share of the warfighting burden. Two divisions operated in I Corps, along with an independent regiment, an armored brigade, a ranger group, and nearly 150,000 militia.[347]

Despite the drawdown, the pace of operations remained high, commensurate with the number of helicopters still in-country. At the height of the Marine aviation presence in spring 1969, three helicopter groups and two SLFs operated in Southeast Asia, totaling 14 squadrons.[348] By early 1971, only MAG-16 with its six squadrons remained.[349] The group's

342 HMM-362 (MAG-36) ComdC, 1–21 August 1969 (21 August 1969), folder 100, U.S. Marine Corps History Division Vietnam War Documents Collection, item no. 1201100017, TTU Vietnam Archive, 5.

343 Col E. R. Brady, USMC, "The Thread of a Concept," *Marine Corps Gazette* 55, no. 5 (May 1971): 37.

344 Provisional Marine Aircraft Group 39 (ProvMAG-39) ComdC, 1–15 October 1969 (6 November 1969), folder 078, U.S. Marine Corps History Division Vietnam War Documents Collection, item no. 1201078433, TTU Vietnam Archive, 4–5; and Smith, *High Mobility and Standdown, 1969*, 344.

345 Smith, *High Mobility and Standdown, 1969*, 344, 356–57.

346 Smith, *High Mobility and Standdown, 1969*, 343.

347 Graham A. Cosmas and LtCol Terrence P. Murray, USMC, *U.S. Marines in Vietnam: Vietnamization and Redeployment, 1970–1971* (Washington, DC: History and Museums Division, Headquarters, U.S. Marine Corps, 1986), 2–4.

348 Report, Marine Corps Command Center, "Status of Fleet Marine Forces," 30 April 1969, Status of Forces file, Reference Branch Collection, HD Archive, 7-3.

349 See tab 33, Report, Marine Corps Command Center, "Status of Fleet Marine Forces," 6 January 1971, Status of Forces file, Reference Branch Collection, HD Archive.

Jonathan F. Abel Collection, Archives Branch, Marine Corps History Division

The final flyby of UH-34Ds in Vietnam. HMM-362 sent off the venerable helicopters—the same type that the unit flew as the first Shufly squadron in 1962—in a retirement ceremony at Phu Bai on 18 August 1969.

128 helicopters were fewer than half the number from two years before.[350] The remaining crews still managed to fly 25,000 sorties in January as the monsoonal weather eased, supporting the 1st Marine Division, U.S. Army, Republic of Korea Marines, and ARVN operations.[351] Marine aviation also supported Operation Lam Son 719, a cross-border operation into Laos, during February and March.[352]

By May, the remaining elements of MAG-16 ended combat operations and began transferring to Okinawa. As of 20 June 1971, no Marine tactical air units remained on South Vietnamese soil after MAG-16 completed its redeployment to Marine Corps Air Station Santa Ana, California. Its exit ended nearly a decade of Marine helicopters operating from bases in the Republic of Vietnam.[353]

Continuity and Change, 1972–75

Although III MAF departed Vietnam in April 1971 and Marine helicopters were freed of direct operations in-country, rotary-wing operations continued to support Viet-

[350] See tab 21-2, Report, Marine Corps Command Center, "Status of Fleet Marine Forces," 6 January 1971.

[351] MAG-16 ComdC, 1–31 January 1971 (12 February 1971), folder 77, U.S. Marine Corps History Division Vietnam War Documents Collection, item no. 120107726, TTU Vietnam Archive, II-1; and Dost, *Marine Corps and Army Helicopter Employment and Attrition Statistics for Southeast Asia Operations from October 1965 through December 1971*, vol. 2, 10, 12.

[352] Robert D. Sander, *Invasion of Laos, 1971: Lam Son 719* (Norman: University of Oklahoma Press, 2014), 109–91.

[353] MAG-16 ComdC, 1–20 June 1971 (20 June 1971), folder 7, U.S. Marine Corps History Division Vietnam War Documents Collection, item no. 1201077275, TTU Vietnam Archive, II-1.

namization in other ways. III MAF Marines became a regional force as the Pacific command's immediate reserve, serving in detachments with the U.S. Seventh Fleet. As such, the helicopters reflected a return to the original vision of the vertical envelopment concept. Composite helicopter squadrons from MAG-36 joined two amphibious ready groups. As the successor to the special landing force, the Marine amphibious unit was the backbone of the landing force. Rotational troops and air helicopter squadrons afloat acting as an air-ground organization deployed in battalion landing teams. Together, these tactical units were on standby to respond to crises, remaining within a week's travel of Vietnam.[354]

The largest such crisis was the Easter Offensive of 1972. North Vietnamese forces launched attacks on 30 March in Quang Tri and Thua Thien Provinces. South Vietnamese firebases and civilian areas were rocked by artillery bombardments while three NVA divisions crossed the DMZ with armor support.[355] The enemy's sudden shift from guerrilla tactics to conventional maneuver warfare caught South Vietnamese commanders by surprise.[356] The Communists seized all major combat bases north and west of Dong Ha within the first 78 hours, and the North Vietnamese controlled the Quang Tri Province by 2 May.[357]

In response, the Americans rapidly built up air and naval forces and sent aircraft, vehicles, equipment, and additional advisors. American leaders hoped the South Vietnamese military could use the extra resources to roll back enemy gains and regain control of Quang Tri Province.[358] Two composite helicopter squadrons from the 9th Marine Amphibious Brigade, the landing forces component of the Seventh Fleet, were offshore at the beginning of May. HMM-165 flying off USS *Tripoli* (LPH 10) and HMM-164 from USS *Okinawa* (LPH 3) were ready to support South Vietnamese Marines with 4 CH-53 Sea Stallions, 14 CH-46 Sea Knights, and four UH-1 Hueys each.[359]

On 13 May, they provided the first direct support as part of a counteroffensive. Aircraft from HMM-164 lifted two battalions of South Vietnamese Marines into attack positions behind enemy lines.[360] The established tactics of Marine helicopter pilots in Vietnam were ill-suited to the operating environment given the enemy's dense network of heavy automatic weapons. Rather than flying above 450 meters, the assaulting helicopters flew at only 10–30 meters, reducing exposure time. In two waves, the squadron moved 60 South Vietnamese Marines in each CH-53 and 20 in every CH-46.[361] Heavy enemy fire in the landing zone hit three

Jonathan F. Abel Collection, Archives Branch, Marine Corps History Division

Marines from 3d Battalion, 26th Marines, board a CH-46 from HMM-164 of SLF B on USS *Tripoli* (LPH 10) in early 1969.

354 Maj Charles D. Melson, USMC, and LtCol Curtis G. Arnold, USMC, *U.S. Marines in Vietnam: The War that Would Not End, 1971–1973* (Washington, DC: History and Museums Division, Headquarters, U.S. Marine Corps, 1991), 2.

355 Cosmas, *MACV: The Joint Command in the Years of Withdrawal, 1968–1973*, 356.

356 Melson and Arnold, *The War that Would Not End, 1971–1973*, 45.

357 LtCol G. H. Turley and Capt M. R. Wells, "Easter Invasion, 1972," *Marine Corps Gazette* 57, no. 3 (March 1973): 22; and Melson and Arnold, *The War that Would Not End, 1971–1973*, 90.

358 Cosmas, *MACV: The Joint Command in the Years of Withdrawal, 1968–1973*, 358.

359 9th Marine Amphibious Brigade (9th MAB) ComdC, 9–30 April 1972 (9 May 1972), folder 53, U.S. Marine Corps History Division Vietnam War Documents Collection, item no. 1201053184, TTU Vietnam Archive, 85.

360 Melson and Arnold, *The War that Would Not End, 1971–1973*, 95.

361 Melson and Arnold, *The War that Would Not End, 1971–1973*, 95.

Jonathan F. Abel Collection, Archives Branch, Marine Corps History Division

South Vietnamese Marines board a CH-46 from HMM-164 for a helicopter assault behind enemy lines in the spring of 1972.

CH-46s and damaged one CH-53 badly enough that the crew abandoned the aircraft.[362]

HMM-164 and HMM-165 successfully transported additional South Vietnamese forces in the coming weeks during operations to defend Hue and take back Quang Tri City and the province.[363] A detachment from the newly formed Marine Attack Helicopter Squadron 369 (HMA-369) joined the 9th Marine Amphibious Brigade in time to begin flying new Bell AH-1J Sea Cobras from ships beginning in June. The attack helicopters interdicted enemy shipping along the North Vietnamese coast, freeing up much-needed fixed-wing aircraft to fly more critical interdiction missions.[364]

On 22 July, Marine helicopters inserted a South Vietnamese battalion northeast of Quang Tri City, the last Marine heliborne assault of the Vietnam War.[365] The NVA offensive stalled once the province was back in South Vietnamese hands. Marine helicopter squadrons assisted RVN forces as needed in the months following North Vietnam's failed invasion. HMA-369's mission continued until 26 January 1973. The following day, the Paris Peace Accords brought a formal end to the United States' combat role in the Vietnam War.[366] By March, the last U.S. military forces were out of the Republic of Vietnam. The Marine Corps' heavy lift helicopters in the region, however, were committed to Operation End Sweep until 30 July, a minesweeping operation in Haiphong Harbor.[367]

[362] 9th MAB ComdC, 1–31 May 1972 (10 June 1972), folder 53, U.S. Marine Corps History Division Vietnam War Documents Collection, item no. 1201053185, TTU Vietnam Archive, III-3; and Melson and Arnold, *The War that Would Not End, 1971–1973*, 96.

[363] Melson and Arnold, *The War that Would Not End, 1971–1973*, 99.

[364] Melson and Arnold, *The War that Would Not End, 1971–1973*, 179.

[365] Turley and Wells, "Easter Invasion, 1972," 29.

[366] An Agreement Ending the War and Restoring Peace in Vietnam, U.S.-DRV, 27 January 1973, UNTS 13295; and Maj George R. Dunham, USMC, and Col David A. Quinlan, USMC, *U.S. Marines in Vietnam: The Bitter End, 1973–1975* (Washington, DC: History and Museums Division, Headquarters, U.S. Marine Corps, 1990), 2.

[367] Dunham and Quinlan, *The Bitter End, 1973–1975*, 44–45.

Afterward, Marine helicopters returned to force-in-readiness status and logged no activity in Vietnam during 1974. The final Marine rotary-wing operations in Southeast Asia were emergency evacuations that took place in spring 1975. In early April, CH-53s from HMH-462 began Operation Eagle Pull, evacuating Phnom Penh as it fell to the Khmer Rouge. Concurrently, North Vietnamese forces launched a final offensive and pushed back ARVN forces to Saigon by mid-April.[368] The 9th Marine Amphibious Brigade received orders on 29 April for Operation Frequent Wind, the emergency evacuation of noncombatants from Saigon. A day later, the Republic of Vietnam fell. The Marines again activated ProvMAG-39 for what would become the largest helicopter evacuation in history. The group consisted of a variety of aircraft from HMM-164 and HMM-165, HMH-462 and HMH 463, HML-367, and HMA-369. Specific numbers vary, but the final operation for Marine helicopters in the Vietnam War rescued more than 1,000 Americans and gave thousands more Vietnamese refugees the chance to start new lives.[369]

Conclusion

General William Westmoreland popularized the idea that the helicopter "came of age" in Vietnam.[370] More specifically for the Marine Corps, the war assured the helicopter's place in the air-ground organization. As one officer posited in *Marine Corps Gazette* in 1977, "If Korea could be considered an elementary school of the air-ground team in learning how to use helicopters in combat, Vietnam was the equivalent of graduate college."[371] Although configured and prepared for amphibious assault missions, Marine helicopters became a land-based force once the Shufly task force went ashore. The scope and intensity of the mission expanded gradually in support of South Vietnamese ground operations against Communist forces.

Marine aviation and infantry elements reunited as an air-ground team in 1965. The combined arms approach that planners envisioned with vertical envelopment proved valid in Vietnam, setting a foundation for discussions about doctrine and force structure for years to come. It could be argued that rotary-wing aircraft strengthened the air-ground team more than had occurred to that point, as those pilots and crews were in closer contact with ground forces than their fast-moving and high-flying fixed-wing counterparts.

While the majority of the squadrons rotating in and out of Southeast Asia were land-based, the 1st Marine Aircraft Wing maintained an amphibious assault presence with a squadron operating afloat as part of the Special Landing Force. Regardless of where the aircraft were based, helicopters made Marine ground operations possible in I Corps. Major General McCutcheon reported in 1967 that the "helicopter has really saved the day for us in Viet-Nam." The aircraft allowed Marines "to position troops quickly and easily. No major operation takes place without them and very few small ones."[372]

With the withdrawal of most American forces by 1973, the Marine air-ground team came to an end in Vietnam. Its substantial experience with the concept, however, pointed the way forward for the Marine Air-Ground Task Force to come.[373] The last years of the war saw a reduced role for rotary-wing aviation and a return of Marine helicopters in the region to the fleet, solely supporting South Vietnamese military forces. The final operations punctuated what countless Marines knew all too well from their time in Vietnam: in times of crisis, helicopter mobility was an invaluable asset.

The demands of the Vietnam War led directly to a modernization of the Marine Corps' helicopter program, placing it in an advantageous position for the coming decades. The first Marine turbine helicopter, the Bell UH-1E Huey, was one of the more versatile rotary-wing aircraft of the war. Sikorsky CH-53 Sea Stallions gave the air-ground team a heavy-lift capability that the original planners of the vertical envelopment concept long anticipated. The Boeing Vertol CH-46 Sea Knight proved itself the workhorse of Marine Corps rotary-wing aviation in Vietnam during the course of nearly a million sorties. One of the more profound changes to Marine aviation was the procurement of a dedicated attack helicop-

[368] Dunham and Quinlan, *The Bitter End, 1973–1975*, 99–124.

[369] Dunham and Quinlan, *The Bitter End, 1973–1975*, 204.

[370] Gen William C. Westmoreland, USA, *Report on Operations in South Vietnam, January 1964–June 1968* (Washington, DC: Government Printing Office, 1968), 121.

[371] LtCol W. J. Smith, USMC, "Preparing Marine Helicopter Pilots for the Next War," *Marine Corps Gazette* 61, no. 2 (February 1977): 27.

[372] MajGen Keith B. McCutcheon, USMC, "Air Support for III MAF," *Marine Corps Gazette* 51, no. 8 (August 1967): 22.

[373] LtCol Kenneth J. Clifford, USMCR, *Progress and Purpose: A Developmental History of the United States Marine Corps, 1900–1970* (Washington, DC: History and Museums Division, Headquarters, U.S. Marine Corps, 1973), 109.

Bell AH-1

The AH-1G Cobra grew out of an emergency requirement in the Vietnam War. Bell Helicopter Company recognized in 1964 that the U.S. Army had an immediate need for a purpose-built helicopter to replace armed UH-1 Hueys. Bell's leadership presented the Army an amalgamated airframe that mated the rear section of the UH-1B with its dependable rotor system and engine to the front half of an earlier scout helicopter concept, creating the HueyCobra.[1] The result was the first attack helicopter, an aircraft that combined speed, agility, a small profile, and a devastating punch.

Defense Department (Navy) 1168731

The AH-1 could easily keep pace with the troop ships it would escort with a maximum cruising speed of 270 kilometers per hour.[2] With a meter-wide fuselage, the two-person crew had unparalleled visibility out a large glass canopy, ahead of which hung a 7.62mm minigun and 40mm grenade launcher on the nose. Short wings mid-fuselage served as mounting points for rocket pods and either 20mm cannon or 7.62mm miniguns, twice the firepower of UH-1B gunships. Deputy Secretary of Defense Cyrus R. Vance Sr. approved the Army's procurement of the Cobra in March 1966. The first airframe arrived in Vietnam in September 1967.[3]

The Marine Corps was also keen to alleviate the burden on its UH-1Es and return them to flying transport and support missions. With improved speed and firepower, the AH-1G promised operational flexibility.[4] The secretary of the Navy approved funding in July 1967 for the three active wings to field a squadron of 24 attack helicopters, but the Office of the Secretary of Defense downsized the order to only 38 aircraft. The first four Marine AH-1Gs to operate in Vietnam arrived in April 1969 and were assigned to VMO-2.[5]

While the AH-1Gs made an immediate impact, it was designed to Army requirements. The interim answer was the Bell AH-1J Sea Cobra. Built to Marine Corps specifications, it featured standard Navy avionics and communications as well as upgraded weapons systems to increase firepower. Critically, the AH-1J was powered by the twin-engine Pratt & Whitney PT6T-3, increasing safety during amphibious operations. The Sea Cobra entered combat testing in early 1971 to impressive results, leading to a Marine Corps purchase of 67 AH-1Js over the next four years. Additional operational experience generated further developments. The AH-1T Improved Sea Cobra entered the Marine inventory in 1977 and later the AH-1W Super Cobra from which the AH-1Z Viper derived.[6]

[1] Stephen Joiner, "Birth of the Cobra," *Air & Space Magazine*, August 2017.
[2] William H. Smith, "HueyCobra," *Army Aviation Digest* 12, no. 5 (May 1966): 14.
[3] Clifford J. Kalista, "The HueyCobra Joins the Army," *Army Aviation* 15, no. 4 (30 April 1966): 13.
[4] LtCol William R. Fails, USMC, *Marines and Helicopters, 1962–1973* (Washington, DC: History and Museums Division, Headquarters, U.S. Marine Corps, 1978), 153.
[5] Fails, *Marines and Helicopters, 1962–1973*, 153.
[6] Bill Siuru, *The Huey and HueyCobra* (Blue Ridge Summit, PA: TAB Books, 1987), 82–91.

Defense Department (Marine Corps) A150961

Vietnamese civilians wait to evacuate Saigon during Operation Frequent Wind.

ter, the AH-1 Cobra. Its addition created a capability that has remained a key component of Corps force structure for more than a half century.[374]

Although statistics and figures offer insights into Marine helicopter operations in Vietnam, they fall short of giving a full accounting of the all-important human component in war. Vertical envelopment was a nascent concept when crews put it to the test in Vietnam. Marine officers and enlisted were the pioneering agents of the helicopter component of the air-ground team in combat. Taking an innovative approach toward greater mobility in modern warfare, they helped make the helicopter essential to the fighting in I Corps. Through exhausting effort, aviators and crew created an enduring legacy for Marine squadrons. Persevering through danger and hardship, they were guided by training and driven by professionalism. Interspersed in the hours of metronomic regularity and tedium were endless examples of bravery and sacrifice. These moments were often the result of the reflexive camaraderie of young men, fueled by a devotion to one another, the Marine Corps, and the nation.

[374] Noah C. New, "Helicopter or Fixed Wing? Both!," *Marine Corps Gazette* 55, no. 5 (May 1971): 26.

Acronyms and Abbreviations

Adv .... Advance
Amtrac .... Amphibian tractor
ARG .... Amphibious Ready Group
ARVN .... Army of the Republic of Vietnam
BLT .... Battalion Landing Team
BuNo .... Bureau Number
Casevac .... Casualty evacuation
CG .... Commanding General
CHECO .... Contemporary Historical Examination of Current Operations
CinCPac .... Commander in Chief, Pacific
ComC .... Command Chronology
COSVN .... Central Office for South Vietnam
CTU .... Commander Task Unit
DIA .... Defense Intelligence Agency
DMZ .... Demilitarized zone
DRV .... Democratic Republic of Vietnam
FMF .... Fleet Marine Force
FMFM .... Fleet Marine Force Manual
HD .... History Division
Helimobile .... Helicopter mobile
HHX .... Heavy Helicopter Experimental
HMA .... Marine Attack Helicopter Squadron
HMH .... Marine Heavy Helicopter Squadron
HML .... Marine Light Helicopter Squadron
HMM .... Marine Medium Helicopter Squadron
HMR .... Marine Helicopter Transport Squadron
HMR(L) .... Marine Light Helicopter Transport Squadron
HMX .... Marine Helicopter Squadron
I Corps .... I Corps Tactical Zone
II Corps .... II Corps Tactical Zone
III Corps .... III Corps Tactical Zone
IV Corps .... IV Corps Tactical Zone

KIA .... Killed in Action
LPD .... Landing Platform Dock
LPH .... Landing Platform Helicopter
LVTP .... Landing Vehicle Tracked Personnel
LZ .... Landing Zone
MAB .... Marine Amphibious Brigade
MABS .... Marine Air Base Squadron
MAF .... Marine Amphibious Force
MAG .... Marine Aircraft Group
MARHUK .... Marine Hunter-Killer Team
MAU .... Marine Amphibious Unit
MAW .... Marine Aircraft Wing
MC .... Medical Corps
MCSN .... Marine Corps Service Number
MCUP .... Marine Corps University Press
MEB .... Marine Expeditionary Brigade
Medevac .... Medical evacuation
MUV .... Marine Unit Vietnam
NLF .... National Liberation Front
NVA .... North Vietnamese Army
PhD diss .... Doctorate of Philosophy dissertation
ProvMAG .... Provisional Marine Aircraft Group
Recon .... Reconnaissance
Rein .... Reinforced
RVN .... Republic of Vietnam
RVNAF .... Republic of Vietnam Air Force
SLF .... Special Landing Force
TTU .... Texas Tech University
UNTS .... United Nations Treaty Series
USA .... United States Army
USN .... United States Navy
USMACV .... United States Military Assistance Command, Vietnam
USMC .... United States Marine Corps
USMCR .... United States Marine Corps Reserve
VHPA .... Vietnam Helicopter Pilots Association
Viet Cong .... Vietnamese Communists
VMA .... Marine Attack Squadron
VMO .... Marine Observation Squadron

Acknowledgments

Assistance from the Marine Corps History Division and the Marine Corps Heritage Foundation made this commemorative volume possible. Thanks to Dr. Edward Nevgloski for the opportunity to write this book. Dr. Brian Neumann made this manuscript better with his keen eye for details. It was a pleasure to work with Jason Gosnell through the editing process. Yvette House provided invaluable oral histories. Alisa Whitley located documents and Samantha Mayo found photographs. Ben Kristy and Carrie Bowers from the National Museum of the Marine Corps contributed useful information about the YN-19 exhibit. The maps are the product of Pete McPhail, with assistance from Bret Rodgers. This effort is dedicated to all Marine rotary-wing pilots, crews, and ground personnel who served in Vietnam.

Adam T. Givens, PhD

Appendix A

AIRCRAFT REFERENCE SHEET

ROTARY-WING

Marine Corps Helicopters

Sikorsky H03S-1 (S-48) utility helicopter
Sikorsky HRS (S-55) utility helicopter
Bell UH-1E ("Huey") utility/armed helicopter
Sikorsky HUS-1 (UH-34D) Seahorse medium-lift helicopter
Boeing-Vertol CH-46 Sea Knight medium-lift helicopter
Sikorsky HR2S-1 (CH-37C) heavy-lift helicopter
Sikorsky CH-53 Sea Stallion heavy-lift helicopter
Kaman HOK-1 (OH-43D) Huskie observation helicopter
Bell AH-1G Cobra attack helicopter
Bell AH-1J Sea Cobra attack helicopter

U.S. Army Helicopters

Bell UH-1B Iroquois ("Huey") utility/armed helicopter
Boeing-Vertol CH-21 Shawnee transport helicopter
Sikorsky CH-54 Tarhe heavy-lift helicopter
Bell AH-1G Cobra attack helicopter

FIXED-WING

Marine Corps Fixed-Wing Aircraft

Cessna OE-1 (O-1) Bird Dog observation aircraft
North American Rockwell OV-10 Bronco observation aircraft
Douglas A-4E Skyhawk light-attack aircraft
Douglas TA-4F Skyhawk Fast Forward Air Controller aircraft (Fast-FAC)

U.S. Air Force Fixed-Wing Aircraft

Boeing B-52 Stratofortress strategic bomber
Fairchild C-123 Provider transport aircraft
Lockheed Martin C-130 Hercules transport aircraft

Republic of Vietnam Air Force Fixed-Wing Aircraft

Cessna L-19 (O-1) Bird Dog observation aircraft
North American T-28 Trojan light-attack aircraft
Douglas AD-6 Skyraider attack aircraft

Appendix B

MARINE ROTARY-WING CHRONOLOGY DURING THE VIETNAM WAR

1962

9 April—Lead elements of Marine Task Unit 79.3.5 (Shufly) arrive at Soc Trang under the command of Col John F. Carey.

15 April—Marine Medium Helicopter Squadron (HMM-362) (Rein), under the command of LtCol Archie J. Clapp, arrives at Soc Trang to begin operations in support of Republic of Vietnam government forces.

22 April—HMM-362 helicopters fly the first combat support missions in Vietnam.

18 June—Marine helicopters first employ Eagle Flight in combat.

30 July—Col Julius W. Ireland relieves Col Carey as Shufly commander.

1 August—HMM-163, under the command of LtCol Robert L. Rathbun, relieves HMM-362 as the operational squadron assigned to Shufly.

4 September—Initial Shufly elements begin relocating to Da Nang in I Corps Tactical Zone.

18 September—HMM-163 conducts first combat operations in I Corps.

20 September—All Shufly elements are in place at Da Nang.

6 November—Marine Task Unit (Shufly) redesignates as Task Element 79.3.3.6.

6 November—LtCol Alton W. McCully relieves Col Ireland as Shufly commander.

7 November—HMM-163 executes the first Tiger Flight reaction force mission in I Corps.

1963

11 January—HMM-162, under the command of LtCol Reinhardt Leu, relieves HMM-163 as Shufly's operational squadron.

19 January—HMM-162 conducts its first combat troop lift in Vietnam.

8 June—HMM-261, under the command of LtCol Frank A. Shook, relieves HMM-162 as Shufly's operational squadron.

2 October—HMM-361, under the command of LtCol Thomas J. Ross, relieves HMM-261 as Shufly's operational squadron.

1964

1 February—HMM-364, under the command of LtCol John H. LaVoy, relieves HMM-361 as Shufly's operational squadron.

19 June—HMM-364 transfers helicopters and maintenance equipment to the Republic of Vietnam Air Force's 217th Helicopter Squadron.

21 June—HMM-162, under the command of LtCol Oliver W. Curtis, relieves HMM-364 as Shufly's operational squadron.

8 October—HMM-365, under the command of LtCol Joseph Koler Jr., relieves HMM-162 as Shufly's operational squadron.

31 December—Fleet Marine Forces, Pacific, changes the designation of Marine helicopter operations in Vietnam from Task Element 79.3.3.6 to Marine Unit, Vietnam (MUV), Task Unit 79.3.5.

1965

17 February—HMM-163, under the command of LtCol Norman G. Ewers, relieves HMM-365 as Marine Unit, Vietnam's operational squadron.

9 March—Marine Unit, Vietnam, is placed under operational control of the 9th Marine Expeditionary Brigade (9th MEB) and redesignated Marine Aircraft Group 16, under the command of Col John H. King Jr. and based at Da Nang Air Base. HMM-163 remains in direct support of ARVN I Corps.

9 March—HMM-162, under the command of LtCol Oliver Curtis, arrives at Da Nang.

13 April—A detachment from HMM-162 of 10 UH-34D Seahorses is established at Phu Bai.

3 May—Six armed Bell UH-1Es of LtCol George F. Bauman's Marine Observation Squadron 2 (VMO-2) arrive at Da Nang, the first Marine helicopter gunships in the Republic of Vietnam.

11 May—The 1st Marine Aircraft Wing (Adv) (1st MAW), under the command of MajGen Paul J. Fontana, is established at Da Nang Air Base.

15 May—HMM-365, under the command of LtCol Koler, relieves HMM-162 at Da Nang.

24 May—BGen Keith B. McCutcheon relieves MajGen Fontana as commanding general of 1st MAW (Adv).

24 May—HMM-161, on board USS *Iwo Jima* (LPH 2) and under the command of LtCol Gene W. Morrison, transfers to 1st MAW from MAG-13.

12 June—HMM-161 relocates to Phu Bai airfield from *Iwo Jima*.

21 June—HMM-261, under the command of LtCol Mervin B. Porter, relieves HMM-163 at Da Nang. LtCol Ewers's HMM-163 becomes the Special Landing Force (SLF) helicopter squadron and boards *Iwo Jima*.

1 August—HMM-361, under the command of LtCol Lloyd F. Childers, relieves HMM-365 at Da Nang.

26 August—MAG-16, now under the command of Col Thomas J. O'Connor, relocates from Da Nang Air Base to Marble Mountain Air Facility, Da Nang.

1 September—MAG-36, under the command of Col William G. Johnson, arrives in the Republic of Vietnam, giving 1st MAW two aircraft groups. MAG-36's rotary-wing elements include: HMM-362 (LtCol James Aldworth), HMM-363 (LtCol George D. Kew), HMM-364 (LtCol William R. Lucas), and VMO-6 (LtCol Robert J. Zitnik). The group is headquartered at the newly built Ky Ha Air Facility at Chu Lai.

12 September—MAG-36's squadrons begin operations.

28 September—HMM-363 from MAG-36 and under the command of LtCol Kew relieves a detachment of HMM-161 from MAG-16 at Qui Nhon.

11 October—HMM-263, under the command of LtCol Truman Clark, arrives at Marble Mountain and reports to MAG-16. Personnel from HMM-163, the SLF helicopter squadron, redeploy to Marine Corps Air Station Futenma, Okinawa.

11 October—HMM-261, under the command of LtCol Porter, transfers from MAG-16 and relieves HMM-163 on board *Iwo Jima*. HMM-261 transfers to USS *Valley Forge* (LPH 8) within days.

1966

4 January—HMM-163, under the command of LtCol Charles A. House, transfers from MAG-16 and relieves HMM-161 at Phu Bai.

6 January—HMM-261 transfers from *Valley Forge* to MAG-36 and relieves HMM-361 at Ky Ha. LtCol Aldworth's HMM-362, in turn, boards *Valley Forge* as the SLF helicopter squadron.

8 March—The first Boeing-Vertol CH-46 Sea Knight squadron, HMM-164, arrives at Marble Mountain under the command of LtCol Warren C. Watson and reports to MAG-16.

27 March—Col Richard M. Hunt relieves Col O'Connor as commanding officer of MAG-16.

15 April—HMM-364, under the command of LtCol Daniel A. Somerville, transfers from MAG-36 and relieves HMM-362 as the SLF helicopter squadron on board USS *Princeton* (LPH 5).

16 May—MajGen Louis B. Robertshaw relieves now MajGen McCutcheon as commanding general of 1st MAW.

23 May—HMM-265, under the command of LtCol Herbert E. Mendenhall, relieves HMM-263 at Marble Mountain. HMM-265 is the second CH-46 squadron from MAG-16.

26 May—HMM-361, under the command of LtCol McDonald D. Tweed, relieves MAG-36's HMM-261 at Ky Ha.

4 July—HMM-364 transfers from MAG-13 as the SLF helicopter squadron on board *Princeton* and relieves HMM-361 ashore at Ky Ha. HMM-363 transfers from MAG-36 and relieves HMM-364 on board *Princeton*.

15 July—MAG-16 establishes a forward headquarters at Dong Ha to support ground operations in northern Quang Tri Province. Detachments of CH-46 Sea Knights and UH-1 Hueys from HMM-164 and VMO-2, respectively, are the first to arrive.

29 July—HMM-263, under the command of LtCol Jerome L. Goebel, relieves HMM-163 as a MAG-16 squadron.

9 August—MAG-16 reinforces its forward headquarters at Dong Ha with a detachment of UH-34 Seahorses from HMM-263.

24 August—Col Victor A. Armstrong relieves Col Johnson as commanding officer of MAG-36.

28 September—HMM-362 relieves HMM-363 as the SLF helicopter squadron on board *Iwo Jima*. HMM-363 comes ashore from *Iwo Jima* and returns to MAG-36.

3 October—HMM-165, a squadron of CH-46s under the command of LtCol William W. Eldridge Jr., relieves MAG-36's HMM-364 at Ky Ha.

16 October—Col Kenneth L. Reusser relieves Col Hunt as commanding officer of MAG-16.

28 October—HMM-163, under the command of LtCol Rocco D. Bianchi, relieves MAG-16's HMM-161 at Phu Bai. HMM-161 redeploys to the United States.

22 November—Col Frank M. Hepler relieves Col Reusser as commanding officer of MAG-16.

4 December—HMM-262, under the command of LtCol Ural W. Shadrick, arrives in Vietnam as a MAG-36 squadron at Ky Ha.

1967

8 January—A detachment from HMH-463, under the command of LtCol William R. Beeler and part of MAG-16, receives the first four Sikorsky CH-53A Sea Stallions at Marble Mountain.

8 January—A detachment of 12 UH-1s from VMO-3, under the command of Maj Kyle W. Townsend, arrives at Phu Bai and reports to MAG-16.

19 January—HMM-362, under command of LtCol Marshall B. Armstrong, comes ashore from *Iwo Jima* as the SLF helicopter squadron and relieves MAG-36's HMM-361 at Ky Ha. HMM-363 from MAG-36 becomes the SLF helicopter squadron on board *Valley Forge*.

19 February—MAG-16's HMM-263, under the command of LtCol Edward K. Kirby, redeploys to Okinawa from Marble Mountain.

29 March—Col Orlando S. Tosdal relieves Col Armstrong as commanding officer of MAG-36.

4 April—HMM-363, under the command of LtCol Kenneth H. Huntington, transfers from the SLF to MAG-16 at Marble Mountain.

15 April—HMM-363 relocates to MAG-16 forward headquarters at Dong Ha from Marble Mountain.

15 April—Commander in Chief, Pacific, commits a second SLF to Vietnam. HMM-263, under the command of LtCol Kirby, becomes the helicopter squadron for SLF Alpha and operates from USS *Okinawa* (LPH 3). HMM-164, under the command of LtCol Rodney D. McKitrick, becomes the helicopter squadron for SLF Bravo and operates from on board *Princeton*.

16 April—MAG-36's HMM-262, under the command of LtCol Shadrick, relocates to Marble Mountain from Ky Ha.

20 April—MAG-16's HMM-265, under the command of LtCol Beeler, relocates to Phu Bai from Marble Mountain.

22 April—Col Samuel F. Martin relieves Col Hepler as commanding officer of MAG-16.

3 June—MajGen Norman J. Anderson relieves MajGen Robertshaw as commanding general of 1st MAW.

13 June—HMM-263, under the command of LtCol Kirby, transfers from SLF Alpha to MAG-36 at Ky Ha.

28 June—HMM-362, under the command of LtCol Nick J. Kapetan, transfers from MAG-36 and becomes the helicopter squadron for SLF Alpha on board *Okinawa*.

2 July—Col Frank E. Wilson relieves Col Tosdal as commanding officer of MAG-36.

12 July—MAG-16's HMM-265 (LtCol Beeler) relieves HMM-164 (LtCol McKitrick) as the helicopter squadron for SLF Bravo. HMM-164 comes ashore as a MAG-16 CH-46 squadron at Phu Bai.

21 July—HMM-361 (Maj Homer A. Bruce) and HMM-363 (LtCol Robert Lewis Jr.) switch bases of operations: HMM-361 to Dong Ha and HMM-363 to Marble Mountain.

23 August—HMM-262 (Maj Gregory A. Corliss) transfers from MAG-36 to relieve HMM-265 (LtCol Beeler) on board USS *Tripoli* as the helicopter squadron for SLF Bravo. HMM-265 transfers to MAG-36 at Marble Mountain.

31 August—MajGen Anderson, commanding general of 1st MAW, restricts all CH-46 flight operations to emergency only after a series of fatal crashes of Sea Knights caused by the disintegration of tail pylons.

3 September—HMM-361, under the command of Maj Bruce, relocates to Marble Mountain from Dong Ha.

5 September—Col Edwin O. Reed relieves Col Martin as commanding officer of MAG-16.

9 September—HMM-163 (LtCol Walter C. Kelly) transfers from MAG-16 and relieves HMM-362 (LtCol Kapetan) as the helicopter squadron for SLF Alpha on board *Okinawa*.

4 October—VMO-6, under the command of LtCol William J. White, is the first MAG-36 squadron to relocate to Phu Bai from Ky Ha where it can better support 3d Marine Division operations.

15 October—Col Wilson, MAG-16 commander, displaces his group headquarters to Phu Bai from Ky Ha. Ky Ha is redesignated MAG-36 (Rear) and Quang Tri becomes MAG-36 (Alpha).

16 October—HMM-164 (LtCol Robert F. Rick), HMM-362 (LtCol Richard W. Cline), and VMO-3 (LtCol Glenn R. Hunter) transfer from MAG-16 to MAG-36. MAG-16 receives HMM-265 (LtCol Beeler).

30 October—HMM-163, under the command of Maj Frederick A. Rueckel, transfers from SLF Alpha to MAG-36 (Alpha) at Quang Tri.

30 October—HMM-263 (Maj James C. Robinson) relocates to Phu Bai from Ky Ha and prepares to combine with HMM-364 (LtCol Louis A. Gulling) before its colors are returned to the United States.

16 November—HMM-361, under the command of LtCol Daniel M. Wilson, transfers from MAG-16 to SLF Alpha on board *Iwo Jima*.

1968

10 January—MAG-36's HMM-165 (LtCol Richard E. Romine) relieves HMM-262 (LtCol Melvin J. Steinberg) as the helicopter squadron for SLF Bravo. HMM-165 embarks on *Valley Forge* and HMM-262 transfers to MAG-36 at Quang Tri.

11 February—MAG-16's HMM-363 (LtCol Frankie E. Allgood) relieves HMM-361 (LtCol Wilson) as the SLF Alpha helicopter squadron on board *Iwo Jima*. HMM-361 goes to MAG-16 at Marble Mountain.

1 March—VMO-3 redesignates as HML-367. It remains under the command of LtCol Glenn R. Hunter at Phu Bai.

3 March—HMM-164 (LtCol Rick) relieves HMM-165 (LtCol Romine) as the helicopter squadron for SLF Bravo.

16 March—HML-167, a new UH-1 Huey squadron under the command of Maj Robert C. Finn, activates at Marble Mountain as part of MAG-16.

14 April—HMM-363 (Maj Duwayne W. Hoffert) transfers from SLF Alpha to MAG-36 to relieve HMM-362 (Maj Walter H. Shauer Jr.) at Phu Bai. HMM-362 boards *Iwo Jima* as the helicopter squadron for SLF Alpha.

16 April—1st MAW activates ProvMAG-39 at Quang Tri under the command of Col John E. Hansen. It is stood up with three squadrons from MAG-36: VMO-6 (Maj Bertram A. Maas), HMM-163 (LtCol Richard G. Courtney), and HMM-262 (LtCol Steinberg).

1 May—Col Bruce J. Matheson relieves Col Wilson as commanding officer of MAG-36.

17 May—HMM-161 (LtCol Paul W. Niesen) relieves ProvMAG-39's HMM-163 (Col Richard G. Courtney) at Quang Tri. HMM-163 transfers to MAG-16 to relieve HMM-361 (Maj Forrest W. Crone) at Marble Mountain. HMM-361 returns to the United States.

16 June—HMM-265 (LtCol Robert J. Edwards) relieves HMM-164 (LtCol Rick) as the helicopter squadron for SLF Bravo on board *Valley Forge*. HMM-164 transfers to MAG-16 at Marble Mountain.

22 June—MajGen Charles J. Quilter relieves MajGen Anderson as commanding general of 1st MAW.

1 July—LtCol Niesen relieves Col Hansen as commanding officer of ProvMAG-39.

5 July—Col Walter Sienko relieves LtCol Niesen as commanding officer of ProvMAG-39.

22 July—HMM-362 (Maj Shauer) relieves HMM-363 (LtCol Hoffert) as the helicopter squadron for SLF Alpha on board *Princeton*.

19 August—SLF Bravo departs the Republic of Vietnam for Subic Bay, Philippines. HMM-265, under the command of LtCol Roy J. Edwards, transfers from SLF Bravo to MAG-16.

22 August—HMH-462, with LtCol Ronald E. Nelson commanding, arrives from the United States with Sikorsky CH-53 Sea Stallions and reports to MAG-36.

31 August—HMM-163 transfers from MAG-16 and redeploys to the United States.

1 September—SLF Bravo returns off the coast of Vietnam from Subic Bay. HMM-165, under the command of LtCol George L. Patrick Jr., becomes the SLF Bravo helicopter squadron on board *Tripoli*.

6 September—HMM-363 (Maj James L. Harrison) relieves HMM-362 (Maj Shauer) as the helicopter squadron for SLF Alpha. HMM-362 transfers to MAG-16.

13 September—Col Warren L. MacQuarrie relieves Col Reed as commanding officer of MAG-16.

30 September—HMM-265, under the command of LtCol Richard L. Yanke, transfers from MAG-16 to MAG-36.

29 November—HMM-164, with LtCol Richard T. Trundy in command, is assigned as the SLF Bravo helicopter squadron on board *Tripoli*.

5 December—HMM-165, with LtCol George L. Patrick in command, transfers from SLF Bravo to MAG-16 at Marble Mountain.

7 December—HMM-362 (LtCol Jack E. Schlarp) relieves HMM-363 (Maj Timothy J. Cronin Jr.) as the SLF Alpha helicopter

squadron on board *Okinawa*. HMM-363 transfers to MAG-36 at Phu Bai.

10 December—HMM-364, with LtCol Merlin V. Statzer in command, transfers to MAG-16 at Marble Mountain from MAG-36.

1969

19 January—HMM-263, with LtCol Robert F. Hofstetter commanding, arrives from the United States and is assigned to MAG-16 at Marble Mountain.

26 January—HMM-362, with LtCol Schlarp commanding, transfers from SLF Alpha to the III Marine Amphibious Force (III MAF). HMM-362 remains on board *Okinawa*. SLF Alpha sails to Subic Bay.

13 February—HMM-362 returns to SLF Alpha operational control, now designated the III MAF mobile reserve force afloat in anticipation of an enemy offensive during the Tet holiday.

1 March—SLF Alpha recommences operations off the coast of Vietnam.

7 March—Col Edward A. Parnell relieves Col Sienko as commanding officer of ProvMAG-39.

13 March—LtCol Floyd K. Fulton Jr. relieves Col MacQuarrie as commanding officer of MAG-16.

10 April—The first Marine Bell AH-1G Cobra attack helicopters arrive at Da Nang as part of VMO-2, under the command of LtCol Clark S. Morris.

3 May—SLF Bravo returns from Subic Bay. HMM-164, with LtCol Trundy in command, transfers from MAG-36 to SLF Bravo on board *Valley Forge*.

16 May—LtCol Herbert J. Blaha relieves Col Matheson as commanding officer of MAG-36.

25 May—HMM-362, under the command of LtCol Schlarp, transfers from SLF Alpha to MAG-36 at Phu Bai. SLF Alpha departs for Subic Bay.

10 July—Col Noah C. New relieves LtCol Blaha as commanding officer of MAG-36.

11 July—MajGen William G. Thrash relieves MajGen Quilter as commanding general of 1st MAW.

1 August—HMH-361, under the command of LtCol Kermit W. Andrus, returns to the Republic of Vietnam as a heavy helicopter squadron and is assigned to MAG-36 at Phu Bai.

13 August—HMM-165 (LtCol Thomas E. Raines) transfers from MAG-16 to SLF Bravo to relieve HMM-164 (LtCol Trundy) on board *Valley Forge*. SLF Bravo departs and sails to Okinawa. HMM-164 transfers to MAG-16 at Marble Mountain.

18 August—HMM-362 (LtCol Schlarp) flies the last UH-34Ds in Vietnam in a retirement ceremony at Phu Bai. The squadron leaves the Republic of Vietnam three days later and redesignates as a heavy helicopter squadron.

12 September—SLF Bravo returns from Okinawa. HMM-164, under the command of LtCol Trundy, transfers from MAG-16 to SLF Bravo and operates from USS *New Orleans* (LPH 11).

26 September—HMH-361, under the command of LtCol Andrus, transfers from MAG-36 to MAG-16 at Marble Mountain.

1 October—Col James P. Bruce relieves LtCol Fulton as commanding officer of MAG-16.

12 October—VMO-6 (LtCol Albert K. Charlton) transfers control from ProvMAG-39 to III MAF and then to the commanding general of 9th Marine Amphibious Brigade.

15 October—HMM-161 (Maj Richard W. Carr) and HMM-262 (Maj Donald J. Meskan) transfer from ProvMAG-39 to MAG-36 at Phu Bai. Commander of ProvMAG-39, Col Owen V. Gallentine, assumes command of MAG-36 at a change of command ceremony at Phu Bai the next day.

21 October—HMM-164, under the command of LtCol Trundy, departs the Republic of Vietnam on board *New Orleans* and redeploys to Okinawa.

31 October—MAG-36 transfers its helicopter squadrons to MAG-16 and redeploys to Okinawa. HMM-161 (Maj Carr), HMM-262 (Maj Meskan), and HML-367 (LtCol Warren G. Cretney) transfer to MAG-16 control but remain at Phu Bai.

7 December—HML-367 (LtCol Cretney) moves from Phu Bai to Marble Mountain.

17 December—MAG-16 realigns its three tactical squadrons: HML-367 (LtCol Cretney) transfers its UH-1Es to HML-167 (LtCol John E. Weber Jr.). VMO-2 (LtCol Stanley A. Challgren) transfers its AH-1G Cobras to HML-367. As a result, HML-367 operates UH-1s, HML-167 operates AH-1s, and VMO-2 operates North American Rockwell OV-10 Broncos.

1970

1 February—HMH-361, under the command of Maj Richard A. Govoni, transfers from MAG-16 to MAG-56 and redeploys to the United States.

8 March—Col Haywood R. Smith relieves Col Bruce as commanding officer of MAG-16.

15 August—HMM-161, under the command of Maj Lewis J. Zilka, redeploys to the United States.

4 October—Col Lewis C. Street III relieves Col Smith as commanding officer of MAG-16.

1971

25 February—HMM-364, under the command of LtCol Neil R. Vanleeuwen, redeploys to the United States.

2 March—The first Bell AH-1J Sea Cobras arrive in the Republic of Vietnam and are assigned to HML-367, under the command of LtCol Clifford E. Reese.

13 May—HMM-262 (LtCol Frank K. West Jr.) and HMM-263 (Maj Dennis N. Anderson) detach from MAG-16 and redeploy to the United States.

29 May—HMH-463, under the command of Maj Myrddyn E. Edwards, detaches from MAG-16 and redeploys to the United States.

2 June—HML-367, under the command of LtCol Clifford E. Reese, transfers from MAG-16 to MAG-36 and redeploys to Okinawa.

10 June—HML-167, under the command of LtCol Richard J. Blanc and the last operational Marine helicopter squadron based inside the Republic of Vietnam, ceases operations there and transfers from 1st MAW to 2d MAW.

20 June—MAG-16, under the command of Col Street, transfers to 3d MAW and redeploys from the Republic of Vietnam.

1972

1 April—HMM-165, under the command of LtCol Paul L. Moreau, sets sail for Vietnam on board *Tripoli* in reaction to the NVA spring offensive. The squadron is part of 9th MAB, the Marine contingent of the U.S. Navy's Seventh Fleet, Amphibious Ready Group (ARG) Alpha and composed of 31st Marine Amphibious Unit (31st MAU) and Battalion Landing Team Bravo (BLT Bravo).

11 April—III MAF forms 33d MAU, consisting of BLT 1/4 and HMM-164 (LtCol Edward C. Hertberg), for operations in Vietnam under 9th MAB.

28 April—HMM-164 sails with ARG Bravo on 16 April on board *Okinawa* and joins 9th MAB in the Gulf of Tonkin. The squadron contains a detachment from HML-367.

5 May—HMM-165 transfers from 31st MAU to 33d MAU and sets sail for Subic Bay on board the *Triploli*.

28 May—HMM-165 returns to the Gulf of Tonkin from Subic Bay and transfers to 31st MAU from 33d MAU.

29 May—HMM-164 transfers from 31st MAU to 33d MAU and departs Vietnamese waters for Subic Bay on board *Okinawa*.

10 June—HMM-164 returns to Vietnamese waters and relieves HMM-165 as helicopter squadron for 31st MAU. HMM-165 transfers to 33d MAU and departs the Gulf of Tonkin for Okinawa on board *Tripoli*.

16 June—HMA-369, under the command of Maj Dawson P. Hansen, transfers from MAG-36 to 33d MAU on board USS *Denver* (LPD 9) in the Gulf of Tonkin. The squadron is to interdict NVA shipping off the coast with AH-1J Sea Cobra Marine hunter-killer (MARHUK) teams.

23 June—HMM-165, now under the command of LtCol Charles H. F. Egger, returns to Vietnamese waters on board *Tripoli*.

1 July—HMM-164 departs Vietnamese waters for Hong Kong on board *Okinawa*.

10 July—HMM-164 returns to Vietnamese waters on board *Okinawa*.

1973

29 January—HMA-369, with Maj David L. Ross in command, ends MARHUK operations off of the Vietnamese coast and transfers to MAG-36 at Okinawa.

12 March—Marine helicopter squadrons participate in Task Force 78's Operation End Sweep, the demining of Haiphong Harbor. HMH-463 (Maj John Van Nortwick) and a detachment from HMM-164 (LtCol Donald E. Schneider) are on board USS *Inchon* (LPH 12). A detachment from HMH-463 is on board USS *Cleveland* (LPD 7). HMM-164 is on board *Iwo Jima*. HMM-165 (LtCol Egger) is on board *New Orleans*.

18 July—HMH-463 (Maj William J. Smith) departs Vietnamese waters and sails to Subic Bay on board *Inchon*. HMM-165 (LtCol Arthur B. Colbert) departs Vietnamese waters and sails to Subic Bay on board *Tripoli*.

1974

No Marine Corps helicopter squadrons in support of Vietnam operations during 1974.

1975

3 March—HMH-462, under the command of LtCol James L. Bolton, transfers to ARG Alpha (Task Group 76.4) for the evac-

uation of U.S. citizens from Phnom Penh, Cambodia, in Operation Eagle Pull.

26 March—HMH-463, under the command of LtCol Herbert M. Fix, joins 31st MAU (Task Group 79.4) and sails to Subic Bay for Operation Eagle Pull.

3 April—USS *Midway* (CV 41) embarks helicopters from HML-367 (LtCol James R. Gentry), HMA-369 (Maj Richard J. Hooton), and HMM-164 (LtCol Dwight R. Allen Jr.) at Okinawa for Operation Eagle Pull.

12 April—Helicopters from 9th MAB execute Operation Eagle Pull.

13 April—31st MAU/ARG Alpha and HMH-462 (LtCol Bolton) sail to rendezvous with Task Force 76.

19 April—HMH-462 (LtCol Bolton), HMH-463 (LtCol Fix), HMM-165 (LtCol James P. Kizer), HML-367 (LtCol Gentry) transfer to ProvMAG-39 as part of 9th MAB (Task Group 79.1) for participation in Operation Frequent Wind, the evacuation of Saigon.

29 April—Helicopters of ProvMAG-39 execute Operation Frequent Wind, the final U.S. operation of the Vietnam War.

www.ingramcontent.com/pod-product-compliance
Lightning Source LLC
LaVergne TN
LVHW061252100826
845148LV00008B/1106
* 9 7 8 1 8 3 9 3 1 5 2 0 6 *